GW00771469

Arthur James Binks was born in 1938 the eldest of four sons of a West Yorkshire farming family. After leaving school at the age of fifteen he trained as a motor mechanic, followed by two years National Service (deferred until he was twenty-one) and worked for a year running a public works transport section before eventually becoming a commercial repairs garage owner. He married his sweetheart, Iris, and enjoyed a happy marriage lasting forty-one years until her death in 2000.

Later in 2000, now living alone, Arthur, whose hobby was sailing his yacht 'Jessica', heard about an expedition to sail the Pacific and applied to join the crew. At the age of sixty-three, he embarked on a voyage of discovery and the adventure of a lifetime.

In 'Wine, Women and Sailing' he tells the story of how he returned from his adventure, having discovered more than he had bargained for.

WINE, WOMEN AND SAILING

Arthur J Binks

Wine, Women And Sailing

Vanguard Press

VANGUARD PAPERBACK

A CIP catalogue record for this title is available from the British Library

ISBN 1 84386 252 2

Vanguard Press is an imprint of
Pegasus Elliot MacKenzie Publishers Ltd.
www.pegasuspublishers.com

First Published in 2006

Vanguard Press
Sheraton House Castle Park
Cambridge England

Printed & Bound in Great Britain

Dedication

I dedicate this book 'To all the girls I've loved.'

Acknowledgements

My grateful thanks to Shirley Durrant for teaching me so much and for making this book a reality. Thanks also to our mutual friend journalist, John Richie, for his interest and encouragement.

I raise a glass and toast my crewmates and travelling companions for the many good times we shared together.

Introduction

Paradise on Earth

The morning sun is shining down on my tent when the sweet sound of birdsong and lapping of wavelets on the coral beach arouses me. It is far too early to be thinking of taking a shower, instead a swim in the warm Pacific waters promises to be the better option. I rise and stretch my legs with a quick sprint around the large clearing that serves as a village green and playing area for the local children.

I slow to strolling pace as I pass through palm trees to the seashore. The sky is a beautiful azure blue and the view magnificent as I gaze out over the reef to the many lush green tiny mutos (islets) that surround the Isle of Atata. The light warm breeze is from the north so today I choose to take my early morning bathe on the south side of the island where the sea will be warmest. I am not alone even at five o'clock in the morning as the islanders are already out in their small boats netting the fish that they will take to the main island of Tongatapu. There they will sell their catch on the jetty in Nuku'alofa, the capital town of the island group. Other fishermen wade on the reef swinging drop nets around their heads and catching fish for today's meal.

Donning mask and flippers I enter the sea and swim out over the reef amongst shoals of fish. Darting about they create a kaleidoscope of colour - blues, yellows, reds, and greens. There are lobsters and crab for the taking but I leave that job to the expert, my wife Manu. She was still asleep when I left our tent and now she joins me in the water. The fire she has lit above the waterline is already blazing as she busily collects crabs for lunch. At her signal we leave the water to sit beside the fire for a breakfast of mixed fruit salad washed down with coconut milk, all freshly gathered from the bush.

While waiting for a couple of red snappers cooking on wooden skewers over the flames, we chat...

'What a life, could this all be real or is it just a wild

dream?' I ask Manu.

This sense of disbelief often passes through my mind but there is no mistake I am actually here basking in paradise and living the way of a native Tongan. For the first time in my life there is no work waiting to urgently take up my time when I awake each morning. I lie back under the glorious sun letting my mind wander; soon memories flood my mind. I ponder the way fate has played a hand by bringing me here, and of the thousands of miles I've sailed across the ocean; the rivers and rain forests I've traversed and the lives and loves of so many different people I've shared along the way.

Chapter 1

Flight to the Big Adventure

When I first heard about the Pacific sailing project I thought, "What wouldn't I give or do to be able to go on a trip like that?"

Trev Plane, an acquaintance of mine whose day job is as a butcher in Doncaster where he lives but whose passion is sailing, has told me he is planning a trans-Pacific voyage.

Trev, who already has several trans-Atlantic crossings under his belt plus the experience of other long voyages, has recently purchased a fifty-foot sloop in the Caribbean and sailed it to the Dutch Antilles near the coast of Venezuela. He has returned to England after leaving the sloop *Antinea* in a boatyard on the island of Curacao for major alterations to be carried out.

He is advertising for crew to accompany him on his planned trip, in tandem with the yacht *Da Capo*. The departure date for Curacao being only twelve weeks away. I tell Trev I am interested in joining him on the voyage.

In June I completed a trans-Atlantic crossing on the yacht *Now*, belonging to Maggie Livingstone, and have since followed that with several two to three hundred mile voyages on my own yacht *Jessica,* so named in honour of my granddaughter. I am eager to try my hand at a Pacific crossing and now luckily the opportunity has presented itself.

As soon as I express an interest to Trev he invites me to join the crew, initiating what proves to be a most exciting experience and one that is to totally change my life.

Despite my initial eagerness to participate in the adventure I begin to feel scared at what I may be letting myself in for; cautiously now I weigh things up in my mind for days before making the call confirming my decision.

"Yes! I will go and that is my final decision."

From the moment I inform a delighted Trev of my intention I bubble with excitement and adrenaline courses through my veins until I am well beyond the point of no return. Even though I am determined to go and nothing and no one can stop me I get in touch with my two sons to see what they think; they both respond similarly.

'Why ask us now? You've never bothered before. Bugger off and enjoy yourself.'

I have their blessing.

There are only eleven weeks in which to make all the preparations and more things to sort out seem to crop up constantly adding to my "list to do". I discover that trying to sort out a year of your life months in advance is no mean feat.

The proposed crews of *Antinea* and *Da Capo* need to have a get-together and then to discuss any queries that may arise from that meeting. So this weekend I collect Trev from his home and drive us both to Mobberly in Cheshire where his friend Adrian lives. Ady, as he is known, owns and skippers the yacht *Da Capo*. He's a married man with three children and aged in his mid-forties. His home is a converted farm at the end of a busy airport runway and it is from here that he runs his business as a roofing contractor. At our first meeting I think…

"Here's a bloody mischievous rogue if ever I've seen one."

The three of us go down to the local pub and drink a few pints of ale before travelling into town to meet with the other volunteer crew at a restaurant. There are two women and three blokes: Sue and Coral and Tony, Don, and Tom. After introducing ourselves we order our meals, have a good natter and as we eat we sink several bottles of wine. I discover bits of background about each of the newcomers.

Sue Lane is single and I'd guess her to be about fifty. She is, I would say, about five foot and six inches tall and of average weight with auburn-coloured hair. Coral is only about a year or so younger and a frumpily-dressed spinster. Tall with long naturally blonde hair she seems a good sport. Tony is a married man from York and a bit older, around about his late fifties; he's medium height for a man and well-groomed and well-spoken; while Don, a retired, married English shoe manufacturer, is of a similar age; his wife, another Sue, may join the crew later. In appearance he reminds me of Yasser Arafat, probably because of his beard. Tom, a Welshman, is a short, greying, fifty-something divorce' and I am soon of the opinion that he is un-streetwise and naïve. They will all join the voyage at different ports along the route.

After the good meal and copious amounts of wine we are in the mood to try anything. The eight of us return to Ady's place where he leads us into a building that looks like a cow shed from the outside but on entering we find it houses a large heated swimming pool. We select items from swimming kit that Ady keeps in the changing room of the converted outbuilding.

Splashing around in the pool for an hour or so we get to know each other a bit more before we are ready to get our heads down for the night; Ady shows us into his house.

The next morning over breakfast we have a discussion and are briefed on the subject of things we should take along on the expedition before we all jump into vehicles to leave Mobberly and head separately back to our own home towns where we will get on with our preparations for the trip. I have plenty to think about on the journey and much more to add to my list so I make notes: spare parts, books to read, favourite tapes, suitable clothes to get, and many other pre-voyage tasks.

I arrange a medical check and at the same time am given so many vaccinations that I feel like a second-hand pincushion. A mammoth shopping trip includes buying numerous medical items to build a comprehensive first aid kit. Trev's wife Carole attends to booking flights via Holland and Aruba to Curacao for Trev, Tom and me who are to crew *Antinea* on the first leg of the trip. This allows me time to visit my close family and friends to say farewell as the departure date draws nearer; finally the big day arrives.

Kev, my eldest son, and Jess, my granddaughter, come to Scarborough railway station to see me off; my last glimpse from the train window is of Jess sobbing her heart out on the platform. I am missing her already.

Trev meets me on time at Doncaster where I am to stay at his home for the night; later that evening we are joined by Tom and after a grabbing a few short hours of sleep we are ready to leave for the airport by 0500 hours.

The taxi ride to Hull is a hairy experience. It is snowing heavily and the ground is already thickly coated. The driver skids dangerously close to the gatepost as we leave Trev's driveway and yet the idiot continues to speed.

Surprisingly we do reach the airport safely and get our bags into the waiting area where an airline official advises us that the flight is delayed for at least an hour and a half leaving us with extra time on our hands. We approach baggage check-in with hearts in mouths, being aware we are all well over the weight limit. When I arrived at Trev's house he told me to empty my bags and remove all the things that weren't important. Then re-pack them with spares and essential equipment only for the trip. I have actually ended up with a hand luggage bag that is heavier than my cargo baggage. Trev asks me to carry it to the check-in desk with one hand to make it appear lighter than it actually is but the check-in operator sees through our little scheme and makes us weigh our hand luggage.

'We're going to get hammered with excess baggage charges,' Trev whispers to me and Tom but she sends the bags and cases into the hold without further comment.

To kill time we are drinking a cuppa when my name is called over the tannoy to return to check-in.

'I bet there's been a change of heart and they won't let my bags through,' I say to Trev and Tom

When I arrive back at check-in I find that it is really Tom they need and not me. The silly little bugger has tied a pair of shoes to the outside of his bag and they have fallen off. This is only weeks after a terrorist tried to enter the USA with a shoe bomb so security is on high alert. A sailor that cannot tie secure knots? I ask you.

In the cafeteria we are handed three vouchers for five pounds each in compensation for the delayed flight and told they can be exchanged for food and hot beverages. After a word with management we get the okay to use them to buy drinks over the bar instead. Tom can't cope with drinking gin and tonic so early in the day so Trev and I feel we just have to help him out and do it for him. We are on our third alcoholic drink when we hear the gate call; as we have just ordered our fourth they will have to wait until we've drunk off.

At the gate I am stopped by an airport official who tells me

I must leave behind a flagstaff I am carrying. Thinking quickly on my feet I begin to limp and tell him.

'I'll be in Queer Street without it.' He apologises profusely and waves me through; I limp and lean heavily on my walking stick.

The flights to Amsterdam and onwards to Aruba in the Caribbean are uneventful. We take off from Hull at 1300 hours and land in Aruba at 1930 hours, four hours behind GMT. While in Aruba I am searched and all my lighters confiscated even though they'd been cleared in Holland, where I had been told that it would be okay to carry them. Obviously some countries are more on the alert than others when it comes to security. Checking through immigration we board the plane and fly on to Curacao.

At baggage collection Trev notices that a lifebuoy he bought in England is missing. It takes half an hour to convince airport staff as no one seems a bit concerned. While we are stuck in the baggage hall Tom is sent to hire a car; he returns telling us he has chosen a smart grey one. We stow our bags in the boot and drive through the darkness to the boatyard in Willemstad.

Chapter 2

Getting Shipshape

Even though it is night the temperature is thirty-two degrees Celsius but the boat has air conditioning making it very comfortable.

I wake up to an absolutely beautiful day. The first task is to stow our gear, then I start work on the boat unblocking one of the heads. Task completed, I take a shower on the diving platform behind the boat.

In daylight we see the smart grey car Tom has hired is in fact a pink one. This gives Trev the inspiration to re-christen Tom as Marvin. Tom likes the name because he thinks it sounds butch but Trev's intention is to liken him to Marvin Gaye.

Taking a trip into Willemstad we stock up with beer from the local supermarket buying 436 cans for US$209, then Trev, Marvin and I have a night in on the boat swigging G and Ts.

New Year's Eve dawns and we go shopping again; the supermarket we found yesterday is equal to Tesco's in England and we are pleasantly surprised. Trev, who is famous for his clumsiness, is true to form today. Every time he reaches out for cans, bottles or packs to add to our stock he manages to knock a whole display pyramid crashing to the ground. Due, I think to the fact that we spent a considerable amount of dollars in the shop the day before, the staff grit their teeth and smile forgiveness. Just as well as if we had to pay for the damages and mayhem he caused we wouldn't ever be able to afford to party again.

We bump into Ady on the marina; he arrived from the airport ten minutes earlier. After helping him stow his gear I ask Trev a question that I know is a sore point with him; not because he is being unfair as in fact he is being just the opposite so far as perks actually fitted to *Antinea* are concerned. He has agreed to pay for such items, or more succinctly as he put it, "The wife has." Trev's wife Carole is flogging her little guts out running their butchery business back in Doncaster while Trev plays in the Pacific Ocean with his boat.

The reason music is a sore point with Trev is this tale he told me earlier. He had visited the boat in Bonaire and sailed it to Curacao taking along a mate from Scarborough who answered to the name of Les. Les had suggested a CD player to Trev that was a very expensive piece of kit but after it was bought they found it had to be linked to a radio. The only radio compatible with it was an even more expensive unit. Les had fitted it but wanted it looking tidy so had shortened the wiring loom but instead of taking a piece from the centre he took it from the end nearest the radio. Too late he found that he had cut the loom almost flush with the radio case and now couldn't reconnect the wires. Ady and me now have to do a bodge job but we manage to get it working. Pleased with our work Ady says to Trev,

'Do you know that this radio is an all singing all dancing state-of-the-art job, it can do anything but give you a wank.'

'That's it then - it's going back! Wanking is the only bloody thing I want it for,' Trev retorts.

We set off for a night on the town calling at a steakhouse on the way. I don't feel very hungry and just have an ice cream which is served by a very nice girl who is sporting a really flashy set of finger nails. Discussing her nail artistry with her inspires the lads to insist I demonstrate my party piece to her. It is the simple illusion of sitting with hands strategically placed on lap in front of trouser flies, fingers interleaved and one fat, disfigured thumb protruding with fleshy pad facing outwards. When she sees my demonstration she can't stop laughing and joins in with our party. On leaving we all get lucky; she gives each of us a hug and a kiss.

It is New Year's Eve so we decide to go wild and drive into the hills to a large, walled village called 'Camp Allegro'. It is famous as the only brothel in the world that is visible from outer space. There seems to be every type of erotic entertainment on offer so I am somewhat surprised when Marvin asks me if I fancy a game of pool. Naturally I decline.

Camp Allegro is made up of small bungalows with a girl sitting in each doorway. One lovely tiny little thing aged about twenty gives me the eye, so in I go. She makes out she is hungry for sex but it turns out her eyes are bigger than her belly; or rather, bigger than her works department to which I am unable to gain entry.

Frustrated I demand to know, 'Do you have a bigger sister?' Getting no response I insist she returns the money I've already paid to be entertained by her.

Meanwhile Trev and Ady have entered two other bungalow boudoirs hoping to satisfy their own particular fantasies. When they finally emerge they each wear the kind of smile a cat that's had the cream might have on its face.

While we are here Trev goes to the airport to collect another crewmember. The bloke had answered an advert for crew placed in England describing himself as well-made and with plenty of experience. When Trev returns to Camp Allegro with Pete in tow we see he is rather more than 'well-made'; in fact he is grossly fat and we all agree he stinks like a skunk. We immediately dub him Fatman, a handle that is to stick as Tom's tag of Marvin has stuck; we are also surprised to find he has flown in from England and not from his homeland of New Zealand as we had been led to believe. Apparently he has been living in England for years.

Another couple of hours is spent by the now five of us, watching the strip shows and other forms of titillation staged at Camp Allegro before we return to the boats.

Fatman, Marvin, Trev, Ady, and me go to Mambo Beach to celebrate seeing the Old Year out and the New Year in. What a place, it is teeming with women and ale flows like water. We suss out Pete, aka Fatman, immediately. His idea of a good night out is to sup ale as fast as anyone is daft enough to buy it for him; we decide to ignore him and drink on our own.

I take a walk down to the water's edge where I come across a young Dutch soldier patrolling the beach and we strike up a conversation.

'I am a conscripted serviceman and this is my posting,' he tells me.

A posting to this Atlantic Paradise, can you believe it? 'I'd sign up right away myself if I thought I could get the same posting,' I reply and I am not joking.

We have an exciting ride back to the boat. Trev drives with the front wheel in the gutter most of the way - and I am sitting over the front wheel. To be on the safe side we had earlier checked up on the local drink-driving laws and were told that there is no such law. For example, a local bloke driving home was so drunk he got out to leave the car and walk but he was approached by two cops and made to get back in the vehicle and drive home because, they warned:

'This road is in a no-stopping zone.'

We spend a lot of time preparing the boat for the first leg of the sailing itinerary; the decks are cleaned and the cabins tidied and the RIB – Rigid Inflatable Boat – given a test-run. The hire car has to be returned but we can only take it back when the punctured front wheel has been changed.

I wonder how that could have happened but I don't have to be Einstein to come up with the answer; after all, a certain skipper drove it wheel in gutter for about ten miles the other night.

After dinner 'the girls' aka Fatman and Marvin are left alone on the boat when Trev, Ady and me go back to the brothel at Camp Allegro for a last fling.

Ady suggests that I take my time and pick out a good one this time; however it only takes me two minutes and what a gorgeous lass I pick. She is a tall, slender, big-breasted Columbian girl, her luxurious long hair cascading over her shoulders. She leads me into her business boudoir and I soon discover that she has learned her trade well; she knows every trick in the book. The hour and a half I spend with her is simply the best.

When Trev and Ady, fed-up of waiting for me, start shouting from outside that it is time we were off I'm very reluctant to leave. The taxi we ordered earlier has had its meter running, so to speak, for the last twenty minutes, waiting for me to emerge from the chicken run. If the lads hadn't become insistent with their shouts of "let's be 'aving yer" the taxi would have been waiting until I either ran out of money or steam. So good is she that put to the test I think the former would have happened before the latter.

This morning Trev prepares us a smashing fry-up breakfast and I have second helpings to replace the nutrients my body lost during my sex marathon last night.

The rain comes and though it only lasts about ten minutes it absolutely bounces down. The rapid change of weather is so exciting I find myself understanding why some people go storm chasing; the effect is so dramatic I am exhilarated. A consolation is that the Caribbean temperatures dry everything up again in no time.

We have decided to eat in town tonight and go to a Chinese restaurant where I have previously drunk in the bar and where I met one of the waitresses now serving us. With a friendly familiarity based on our earlier acquaintance, every time she passes she gives me a prod; meaning to return the compliment I unfortunately misjudge and catch her in a slightly awkward place. The accident has Ady roaring with laughter and on hearing his guffaws the waitress turns, picks up his drink and throws it over him. This episode dampens the party mood like rain on a Whit weekend and we up and leave scurrying rapidly around the three burly bouncers who enter the door at the sound of the commotion.

Returning to *Antinea* at 2130 hours we crank up the engine and are soon on our way motoring down and out of the bay en route for Cartagena.

Chapter 3

Cartagena, Columbia

As we are leaving Curacao in darkness we watch the unusual blue lights; yes, blue lights of Camp Allegro, from many miles distant until they eventually fade out of view. I wonder at the reasoning behind using blue lights.

To get out into the open sea we have to pass through the oldest pontoon swing bridge in the world, the Königin Emma Brug. Seeing it open to allow us through is a fascinating experience. The bridge is very long and built onto canoe-shaped floats. A large float at one end is actually a ship; this pulls the bridge open while pivoting on a hinge at the other end. It is a very slow procedure.

Trev had brought *Antinea* to the boatyard in Curacao to have a number of repairs and installations carried out by so-called expert fitters. From the word go it is obvious that they are no more than a set of boatyard cowboys and as we proceed the dire results of the work they have carried out becomes obvious, proving our initial perception to be correct.

Our auto-helm doesn't work nor do any of the instruments. These boatyard cowboys have caused damage to the wiring when working behind the electric panels.

So it is all manual steering until we reached Cartagena in Colombia. We average 7 knots steering 300 degrees to Aruba. I do first watch, 2300 to 0200 hours, then try to get some sleep but it is so hot that I have a very restless night.

I am fully awake at 0730 hours. We are passing between Aruba and the Peninsular De Paraguana still doing 7 knots with the wind due east. The coast of Venezuela is clearly visible and being my first sight of the South American continent it is a milestone in my adventure.

Our speed has picked up to 9 knots and we are experiencing a comfortable sail. We catch a small tuna that afternoon. I take over the helm at 1630 hours and by 2000 hours Trev and Ady are opening the wine and we start sipping, or is it supping? I am feeling a bit tipsy but still they force more down my neck; that's what you get when you can't keep your mouth shut. I get so bad that I ask them to let me stand down, but no! It is 2230 hours before I finish my stint and by that time I am absolutely blathered. During this watch I've managed to destroy a pair of glasses, one of ten pairs I've brought along.

Just as I am about to go to bed I decide to take in the fishing line for the night, but when it is half-way in I get a bite and land a 9lb tuna which we can have for dinner tomorrow.

After a good sleep I am up like a lark at about 0800 hours; the wind has come behind so we are able to hoist the spinnaker and the speed picks up to 12 knots. The wind then changes to 36 knots increasing our speed but we have already changed the sail back to Genoa. The sea builds up so high that anyone suffering from constipation will soon be completely cured. During this storm we manage to hook and land another 10lb tuna; that's another good meal to look forward to.

Hours later we pick out the Colombian coastline but stay well out because of the many rocks. When it is time to make our approach to the bay entrance I find a narrow passage into the bay very interesting. It has at one time been protected by cannon emplacements at each side and having been well preserved they are still in place. We sail up the long bay dropping anchor just short of the marina at 2100 hours and here we celebrate our trip by getting sozzled on red wine. Up to now the wine has always been good quality but the price we pay varies wildly from place to place; even so the highest price we pay here is always cheaper than it would be for an equivalent bottle back in England.

The temperature this morning is near to 37 degrees Celsius so I laze about a bit until we have tied up in the marina. We give Ady a hand to get his gear and the drink onto *Da Capo* as he has paid for half of the wine and beer. It turns out to be a long hot task only made easier by imbibing copious quantities of ice-cold cans.

I spend a lot of time fixing things on *Antinea*. The boat stern is tied to two large pillars standing aft of us; these are usually occupied by pelicans that seem to stand there on one leg most of the day. When feeding they fly high over the water and then dive straight in seeming always to catch their prey. I've heard that when they age they develop arthritis in their necks due to all the diving and the pain gets too much for them to dive for food, resulting in them starving to death.

The women of Columbia are very pretty; pleasant and friendly too. I take it for granted that they are all of the same character and get mugged for my naivety. We are taking a walk around one night and venture into the red light area to try our luck; we only find one place where all the girls are dog rough and we leave there in a hurry. As we walk along a gorgeous young thing approaches and offers herself to me. The fee that she asks for should have alerted me as it is only the equivalent of about sixty pence, yet I see it as an offer too good to miss. She lets me squeeze the fruit as it were, even before I give her the hard cash. Suddenly a bloke runs up and jumps on my back at the same time breaking and snatching off my gold chain. I can't retaliate as I have my hands full at the time. All the lads are there but it happens so quickly that nobody can do anything, which is maybe a good thing as the locals wouldn't think twice about bringing a knife out.

Fatman too has an amorous experience; we use an alfresco disco bar situated on the city wall and on our first visit made the acquaintance of two very pretty Colombian girls who made it quite clear from the outset that they are lesbians. However, this is of no consequence as they are pleasant company and willing to be dancing partners. To cut the story short, *Fatman* is not in the know and continuously tries to chat them up. Eventually out of sheer desperation the girls give him their hotel phone number. Believing himself to be a whiz kid he rings the number and obtains the name and location of the hotel.

When we are up and about the following morning no one can help but notice the extra space on the boat; finally we realise *Fatman* is missing. He doesn't return until evening when he relates his woeful tale to us, a tale that if it had happened to me I'd have kept to myself.

He took a taxi to the girls' hotel and had the reception staff wake them; being absolutely delighted to see him (his words) they agreed to accompany him to the beach where he treated them to a few beers, before they all lay down to sunbathe. He dozed off to sleep.

Imagine his surprise when he awoke late afternoon to find himself alone and with his face and belly burning as red as ripe tomatoes. The birds had flown but left him with just enough cash for a cab ride back to *Antinea.*

Few people in Cartegena can speak any English, while I can speak only just enough Spanish to break the ice and order beer. Fuel here costs thirty-nine pesos a litre with 300 pesos to one GB pound yet by the locals it is still thought to be too expensive.

Trev and me walk to town one day and as we reach a traffic island we see a hand cart measuring about four by three feet that only consists of framework. The odd thing is that two pairs of legs are hanging out at the rear. We see the same cart the following day and a young couple seated close by are cooking on an open fire; it is then we realise that the cart is their mobile home. We keep a lookout for it after that and see it parked on a highway central reservation with a line of clothes drying between two trees. By now it has been customised and curtains hang from it. We laugh, but it shows the conditions under which some people have to live.

Lucy, Tony's daughter, has joined us during the day; she is to live on Ady's boat and they consummate their new partnership within several minutes of her joining him.

We all stay on the boats that night to have a bit of a party. The following days are spent taking casual walks into town or lazing about drinking wine. The only work I do is to refit some broken screws to the base of the mast.

I am introduced to a new friend Dr Jaimie (for some reason Trev pronounces it Dr *Hymie* although I am never sure why) who is the chief medical officer in Cartagena and has his own hospital. He is a perfect gentleman. Separated from his wife he has a twenty plus-year-old son and sails in his leisure time. He is to do a great deal to smooth the way for us and make our stay here a very pleasant time.

Jaimie accompanies Trev and me to the Pedro District in order for us to try to obtain a ninety amp alternator. The area is packed with anything and everything to do with automobiles -

repair shops exist in abundance with all repairs being carried out on the street. It is like watching an army of ants at work. There are numerous used spares shops no bigger than kiosks and motor factors everywhere we look.

With the help of Jaimie we find the new alternator we require and after getting the vendor to by-pass the control box it is purchased.

On the way back we get another glimpse of how the other half live. We see a large, high hillside covered in shacks with hordes of yelling kids running around. A lot are barefoot and poorly dressed but the women, whatever the family's financial status, are invariably well-dressed and made up. Most of the inhabitants living in these circumstances are so poor that they have to beg or steal to live.

On verges alongside the roads are big log fires with huge vats of stew sitting on them and all day long families come to buy a meal in a bowl. It is certainly a no-go area at night and it is even necessary to stay close together during daylight hours.

The town is airless, stifling; we are gasping for a drink when we return to the boat. It's amazing how quickly dehydration can overtake a body. Dehydration causes tiredness combined with bad headaches similar to a hangover; another sure sign is when your urine looks like treacle.

To re-hydrate, the answer is simple: drink plenty of water and soon your condition will improve. It is advisable to carry bottled water around with you all of the time, which we in our complacency or stupidity failed to do today. We do know the necessity but to our peril chose to ignore it; never again though.

In the evening, on Jaimie's recommendation, we visit the Las Pelicano restaurant; the outing at the current exchange rate costs us each around fifteen GB pounds. We eat three courses and drink as many bottles of wine as we can sink; the owner looks aghast when, after we have consumed twenty bottles, we order yet another. We tell him that we will pay extra from that point which puts a smile back on his face.

It is Sunday 13th January and we have a treat, enjoying an early drink on *Da Capo* before joining Jaimie on his boat at 1000 hours for a sail down the bay taking a short cut out to sea.

The short cut is a bit hairy as a submerged reef about a quarter mile long blocks the way but there is a passé marked by two coloured poles only about six metres apart and Jaimie takes us through with no bother.

Following the same course as when we first came here we sail about ten miles down the coast then through the same fortified passage into the bay. We have a nice trip because now in daylight we can do a bit of sightseeing as we return up the bay to the marina.

Jaimie knew it would be dry, thirsty work so he's put a good stock of ice-cold ale on board; he has even employed a youth who passes out the beer as fast as we can drink it - and that is fast. The lad works full time on the boat in return for which, Jaimie keeps him in food and spending money.

Jaimie later cooks a fine steak dinner that we eat on board *Da Capo;* swilling it down with plenty of wine is a great finish to a day made memorable by the fantastic sail and the superb company.

I spend the following day in town with Trev and Ady, drawing cash from the bank and sending an e-mail to my mate Jim. It is very hot so we cool down with a can or two at an open-air bar where we order tuna salad sandwiches to eat as we sit around telling the tale.

Two young lads come to our table, one of them holding out his hand so we copper-up and are about to hand him a bob or two but he shakes his head and points to the remains of our snack. We pass him the plate and are aghast when both lads wolf the grub down like there is no tomorrow; they must be absolutely starving.

On the way to find our taxi we see a liquor store and stock up on gin and tonic; it is quickly put to good use when at sundown we hold yet another party aboard *Da Capo.* I have gained a reputation as a joke teller and apparently my subtle one-liners are much appreciated. Seemingly, whether it was the amount of booze consumed or not I don't know, but at this particular party I excel myself. Ribs, they say, ached with laughter and I don't think they mean RIBs.

The marina is protected at all times by armed guards, a few

of whom I have made the acquaintance of. Early one morning as I am leaving Ady's boat I meet one of them; the young lad is sitting on the pontoon and appears to be in a lot of pain. I take a look at his leg and see that the ankle is sprained and badly swollen. Returning to *Antinea* I get some ice from the freezer and pack it around his ankle. We then sit together on the pontoon for hours chatting happily together until the swelling goes down and he feels well enough to hobble back to the control office. We get on great guns even with our limited knowledge of each other's language; it's amazing how much can be conveyed with crude sign language.

Another fabulous day dawns and Dr Jaimie calls around to see us and takes me along with Trev and Ady to a gas manufacturer's situated well outside of town. Dr Jaimie seems to have a lot of pull wherever we go and in no time at all our bottle has been refilled. On our way back we call at a warehouse where they sell second-hand parts for boats and Trev buys three brass portholes; he plans to make two of them into picture frames and a mirror from the third for *Antinea.* Trev is quite creative at making things. We see interesting old parts of ancient galleons that have been recovered for sale in the warehouse; it is fascinating to view such artefacts.

There are restrictions about staying in Colombia as indeed there are in most places in the world; one of these being a three-month time limit. Moored nearby is a boat sailed by a German couple who have exceeded their stay; their passports are seized and an $1800 fine imposed. They leave the country a few days later but the incident is not quickly forgotten; we realise that the authorities here mean business. If the treatment they received was meant to serve as a warning to others, from the worried conversations I hear around the marina it has certainly worked.

Around this time I am being kept very busy carrying out repairs on *Da Capo.* I also have to climb the mast on *Antinea* to fit a lightning conductor; this involves moving the VHF aerial. The next task is to visit the airport to collect three new crew members: Don and his wife Sue who are coming to join *Da Capo*, together with Coral who is to join us on *Antinea.* Don's wife is a petite woman with dark hair.

We give them a welcome party on *Antinea* at which I apparently have a good time. I wake with a thick head which clears after drinking plenty of water. I then set off with Trev for the *ferriterias,* ironmongers. We are in need of a tap fitting for some gas bottles he's purchased. The *ferriterias* owner is going into the city and volunteers to take us along but the place he takes us to only stocks welding supplies; out of luck we return to town. We ask around again then hail a taxi to an address we've been given. After travelling for miles we finally reach the shop and this time we are lucky, managing to obtain the correct parts.

On the way there we see many armed soldiers but on the journey back their numbers appear to have doubled. We also see the passengers from several buses being searched; the soldiers have everyone spread-eagled against walls with guns aimed at them. We mention this later to Jaimie who tells us that terrorists are infiltrating the city limits in an attempt to initiate an uprising. Shortly after our experience the government declares war on them.

We have been having a lot of problems with the water-maker that was fitted at the boatyard in Curacao. I end up changing all the pressure pipes dozens of times and it is becoming monotonous. So it makes a pleasant change when on Saturday 19th January there is a yacht race and we take part sailing with Jaimie on his boat.

We make a good start and at the first turning are in the lead by a short margin then we quickly speed ahead; the boat is badly rigged so we have to make a lot of adjustments on the way.

Our beer stock is as high as it had been on the previous sail and we sink a great deal of beer; in fact after the race finishes several crews tell us that they worked hard to try and gain ground on us even though we seemed to be preoccupied with drinking can after can of beer rather than winning the race.

We didn't win. At one stage of the race we were a good ten minutes in front but then Jaimie led us on a wrong course and by the time we re-traced and went around the correct buoy we had dropped behind. Despite our beer intake we did put in a lot of effort and at the post had almost caught up with the eventual winner, a Columbian boat; we are the only non-Columbians in the race.

Reflecting on our close defeat over a post-race beer Jaimie says with a rueful look in his eye,

'It had to be this way, this is Colombia not England; some people expect to win every time and may not have hesitated to shoot anyone obstructing this privilege.'

The crews of both *Da Capo* and *Antinea* go to the Yacht Club for dinner where we enjoy an excellent seafood meal. I chat with Don's wife and contrary to what the others have told me I find her to be a very nice lady. For me this has been another brilliant day.

Both crews get together next morning to pay a visit to the San Philippe Fortress; it is a massive structure but hadn't been capable of stopping Francis Drake sailing up into the bay and bombarding the city to smithereens all those years before.

We spend a lot of time walking around the passages built into the fortress but the odd thing is there are no actual rooms. Dark tunnels link the powder stores and cannons are mounted on parapets. I find some terrific viewpoints for camera shots and take lots of photographs.

After the visit we walk to town in unbearable heat before Trev and me return to the boat to re-hydrate in the best way we know how.

Earlier in Pedro we ordered four new batteries; they arrive and we find they won't fit into the mountings. Again Jaimie comes to the rescue and accompanies us back and soon we have another set. I see at a glance that they aren't of the same quality as the first set but as we are shortly to set sail we will have to make do.

Our next task before setting sail is fraught with difficulty; when we arrived all passports, ship's papers and the crew list had to be taken to immigration. The women in the office were very aloof and officious; they took all the papers from Trev returning all but one; this one the woman placed in a desk top drawer. The paper is of great importance and although Trev requested it back the woman refused. Our best chance of sorting out the problem is to be again accompanied by Dr Jaimie and as usual he insists it is no bother to him to do it.

We go for clearance but are told they need to see the very

paper in question; the woman is adamant that she has never ever seen the document. Jaimie sets about her at once and plays merry hell yet still she maintains she has not seen the document. Jaimie now threatens to report her to her superiors but she still denies having seen it. I think she must have pressed a panic button because a gun-toting guard walks in and stands behind us. Jaimie carries on pressing her but she will not open the drawer. Finally he marches round the counter and pushing her out of the way peers into the drawer himself; there it lies right on top of the drawer's contents; he picks it up and waves it in the air. He is so angry he gives her the best bollocking I have heard in many a year; entertaining too, even the guard turns his head away to laugh at her expense. Problem solved I head into town where I try sending several e-mails but none of them get through.

'What sort of a bloody Mickey Mouse system do they have here?' I fume aimlessly.

Trev gets some carpenter's to *Antinea* to alter a few lockers; they are getting on well with the work too until Fatman has one of his not-so-bright ideas: it is to fit removable dowelling across the front of the lockers. It will cost Trev a bomb for the extra work carried out on an idea that should have been knocked on the head immediately it popped out of Fatman's mouth. It is unnecessary and unworkable. Then there is the problem with employing cheap local labour to consider. They have no modern equipment so while the hourly rate seems very low, the extra time it takes to do the job due to the lack of suitable tools makes the final account four or five times more expensive than it should be.

Soon it is time to prepare for our next voyage. Water tanks have to be filled, dirty clothes and bedding taken for a wash at the local laundry and a new grab rail that Trev has designed, fitted on top of the galley worktop. This proves to be a great success and helps a lot in preventing accidents. Normally in rough weather anyone in the saloon has a difficult time moving around on the high waves, often getting thrown about risking serious injury. This rail is fitted both vertically and horizontally and it can be grabbed in most situations.

Trev and Coral take a taxi into town and fetch back a lot of groceries while I stay behind rigging up the mainsail lazy-jacks.

Later the two crews all go in to town together for a last night out. Ady and I take a short trip to the seedier part of Cartagena for a final look around; it is a well-spent half hour. We encounter one or two women offering to entertain us for a small sum but we decline; instead we treat them to a beer and after an interesting natter we leave them to rejoin the others at *La Pelicano* restaurant.

24th January dawns and everyone is up early. The tanks are topped up at the fuel dock before Marvin and I go to town with our leftover local currency, spending it all on more cans of beer.

Chapter 4

San Blas Islands

Leaving Cartagena at 1030 hours, the wind is a north easterly and couldn't be better. We sail down the bay and out into the open sea on a course of 258 degrees making 8 knots. I stand watch for three hours then go onto the foredeck to top up my all-over tan.

My next watch is 2000 to 2200 hours. When it is over, blow me if I don't start with really bad stomach pains and am unable eat or drink. I retire to my bunk and sleep through until 0830 hours but feel much better when I awake. We have now only another seventy miles to go. The wind is coming from the north so we hoist the spinnaker but soon after there is another wind change so we have to drop the spinnaker and get back to the Genoa. The rest of the trip is fairly uneventful and we sight land at 1630 hours. We are about to enter the San Blas islands; there are dozens of them and every one looks breathtakingly beautiful.

The first group of islands we visit is protected by a long reef; there is a passé through although it is fairly narrow. We enter the passé with hearts in mouths especially when the sounder leaps from a depth of several hundred metres to a mere seven, then, phew, we are safely through and into a lagoon. We still have to feel our way around more reefs and coral heads before we are in safe waters; it takes a fair time before we feel that we are able to drop the hook. There is always a large area to slowly survey to be sure of a safe swinging circle but finally we are secure in ten metres of water.

The first thing I do is to have a skinny dip in the lovely warm water; I follow the dip with an invigorating cold shower. We haven't been here much over an hour when we see the first dugout canoe approaching. There are two Spanish-speaking Indians in it and soon we are being charged a $5 fee which will allow us to stay in their pond for as long as we want. We are later to be visited by other canoes bringing goods to trade and bonny daughters who want to have their photos taken while they sit in the boats giggling.

We decide on a quiet evening with the crew fixing up a lantern in the cockpit and settling down to a roast chicken dinner washed down with the usual copious amounts of wine. By the time the meal is over I am ready for a good sleep, but no chance. My proposed good sleep is ruined by Fatman and Marvin tinkering with the boat's electrics and constantly running the engine.

The natives must have been waiting to see the first signs of life on board as the next morning we are visited quite early by more of them in canoes displaying their wares by holding them aloft. I buy two pieces of cloth embroidered with intricate designs following patterns similar to those used by the Incas; both are fine examples of Indian handicraft.

When the natives have left I go ashore to explore with *Da Capo's* crew; we wade round an island with the water at times reaching up to our waist. The feeling that we are being adventurous is great. In some places we find large conch shells washed up in heaps of several dozen but only one or two are undamaged.

Back at the boat fishermen wanting to sell us fish pay us a futile visit as we still have plenty left. It becomes so hot that I take another skinny dip and am surprised when Coral joins me; she has kept herself apart up to that point but suddenly begins to join in.

There's been no end of trouble with the new batteries of late; they don't seem to be holding the charge even when the engine has been running for hours. As soon as I find time I check them over to discover that Fatman, who fitted them, hasn't tightened any terminal clamps or fittings so we've been lucky not to sustain any serious damage. For a long time to come we are to find many more examples of his half-finished, shoddy jobs.

Ady takes his crew to an inhabited island and is away for hours; he relates to us that the natives were pleased to see them and he and the crew have taken some lovely photos. That night we party on board *Antinea* and the next morning find the foredeck covered in spilled red wine; it is literally everywhere. I set about cleaning it up and although it is hard work I get there in the end. After my deck-cleaning session both crews take to the RIBs and visit another uninhabited island where we find a well containing fresh drinking water. Apparently it is actually seawater that has filtered through the reef and sand but it tastes really good.

Nobody lives full time on the island but while on a walkabout we see the palm trees have all been neatly trimmed and the ground kept tidy. Even dead fronds have been heaped up and burned. We also come across a small bamboo hut containing a four-poster bed complete with mattress; there is no other furniture or any personal possessions in the hut. We are ultimately informed that natives do a stint on the island collecting coconuts and looking after the trees.

Picking up fallen coconuts we drink the milk; Ady has had the forethought to bring a machete so we are able to eat the flesh too. We collect more and carry a few each back to the boats to enjoy later.

After lunch we visit the island of Tiadup where the canoes of trading natives who visited us came from. At first sight it looks deserted but everyone emerges from their bamboo huts as soon as they become aware of our arrival. We have a wonderful time especially when teaching the kids to play frisbee. They bring fresh baked coconut bread for us and we buy several lobsters from them before being shown around their tiny island home of which they are all very proud. I don't think Tiadup can be more than a quarter of a mile in diameter.

Returning to the boats we gather up things to trade with them and revisit our new-found friends; this time we remember to take our cameras.

We photograph the children first but the old chief pushes them out of the way to pose alone making it quite clear that he comes before anyone on the island. Even when I pass lollipops out to the kids he snatches the first one but doesn't know what to do with it so he just stares at it until someone pulls the wrapper off one and gives it a lick; quick on the uptake he gleefully pops it into his mouth.

I've brought some old and in some cases, broken specs,

also lipsticks, perfumes and a lot of cheap jewellery. Earlier Don took a photo of the old chief and he offers it to him but it soon becomes clear that he can barely see. I give him a pair of glasses and fit them on him. He looks at the photo and at first seems startled then grinning from ear to ear he gives me a great big bear hug. His wife comes next and to her I give a lipstick and a brooch, then she stands smiling with lips pouted while I paint them for her.

I am suddenly mobbed by all the young girls but I have something for each of them. I have nothing suitable to give a boy amongst them who looks to be about twelve years old; then I remember the little jewellery pouch I had carried the trinkets in; I hand it to him and he dances about with joy waving the bag around for all to see.

Quite unexpectedly I feel a prod in my back. Turning I see the old chief's wife grinning from ear to ear and wearing his spectacles. I just have to give her a pair of her own but there is a slight problem as the only pair I have left have a frame with only one surviving ear hook yet this doesn't deter her one iota; she is quite happy to wear them at an angle, Eric Morecambe style. From the moment she has them on her face she beams in delight.

We stay until dusk before going back to the boat to finish our day with a curry and plenty of beer.

Out on the main reef we can see the remains of a boat that has missed the passé; it *was* a very large yacht but only the hull remains as it has been completely stripped by the Tiadup Indians for everything to be made use of.

On top of one hut is a solar panel connected to a battery that in turn lights a twenty-one watt bulb inside the hut; it is the only home on the island to be illuminated. There are several more things that have been salvaged from the wreck and put to odd uses. For instance, they have been recycled as cooking utensils and a large oil drum is used as an oven to bake bread for the tiny community.

The island's natives are Kuna Indians. Every island is self-ruling and run by a group similar to a committee. The larger tribes even have their own policemen to enforce tribal laws, while the elders hand out their own punishments. It all seems to work smoothly and crime on the islands is unusual.

Their culture expects girls to become wives as soon as they reach puberty; they don't normally get a choice of partner but have to take the first in line no matter how young or old he may be, yet they all appear happy with this system.

We visit our Tiadup friends again before we leave, to take photos of them dressed in their best clothes and leave them prints downloaded from the computer. We are expecting to see everyone waving us off when the anchors are raised but not one of them appears from out of their bamboo huts.

We move on again sailing on headsails only until we have passed between two large reefs and drop anchor in ten metres of water just off Waisaladup. Although Waisaladup is very tiny it is the ideal place to have a barbecue.

Da Capo's crew go ashore to get the fire going while we prepare some of the food and the next thing I hear I am being called on the VHF to join them quickly, together with my first aid kit. Ady has suffered a bad gash to his big toe. I make all haste to join them and I clean and dress the wound and prescribe a couple of bottles of wine which I help him to drink; he is soon almost as good as new and so am I. We eat a delicious barbecued meal and then get so blathered that I don't even remember getting back to the boat.

As soon as he wakes up this morning Ady comes on board and I am invited to breakfast on *Da Capo*. His idea of fruit dessert is a large bowl of sliced oranges marinated overnight in wine and rum. I am given the lion's share and it is as effective as eating the hair of the dog.

At 1100 hours we look back to the island where we were the night before and see that it is almost under water; there is very little range on the tide here but enough to almost submerge some of the tiny islets.

We are still having trouble with the new batteries; after further testing I find one to be faulty and have to disconnect it, then after raising anchor we set off to an island near the mouth of the Rio Diablo.

There are two small islands close together linked by a bridge; both villages are kept independent of each other and are ruled by separate councils. A Kuna Indian named Fredrico meets us at the landing; he offers to be our guide saying he can speak a little English. On a walkabout he explains a lot about their way of life; it is all very interesting. There are several small stores on the islands to which he takes us and everyone is friendly, their kids following us around everywhere we go. At one village they have a miniature zoo that is home to three small antelopes, two tortoises, and a wild pig. We buy a few things from the very limited choice on offer at the stores before going back to the boats for lunch.

After our meal break we return to pick up Fredrico who guides us to the river in our dinghies. Close to the mouth the river is littered with debris and old tree stumps that have been washed down in the floods. There are also a lot of shallows where we ground several times; the first mile is nothing but mangrove swamps then we are into virgin forest. It is a new and very exciting experience, like heading into the unknown. We see Indian families who have paddled up river in dug out canoes to the many deep pools where they wash their laundry and bathe at the same time. The six groups we see on the trip all appear to be busily enjoying themselves but they take time out to laugh and wave to us as we pass.

Most Indians have little facial hair and the bit that does grow is plucked out by using small fresh water mussel shells as tweezers; Fredrico gives us a little demonstration. After the trip we return him to his island and go back to the boat for a meal of fruit and cream before putting out to sea again. We sail along the Isthmus of Panama back into the San Blas to the tiny island Nusatupu (Rat Island) off the Rio Sidra.

The island is densely populated with bamboo huts thatched with palm tree leaves; no hut is more than three feet from the next. While visiting we call on the headman who takes us round his village; there are lots of very friendly children all trying to sell something and I buy a small balsa carving for $1 then find it to be full of wood lice and have to throw it away.

During our walk I notice two little girls following me around then they take hold of my hands; I am not taking any particular notice of them and they go away for a time but when they return they are wearing different clothes that I can only describe as very much less discreet than those they were wearing before. They try all sorts of antics to get my attention and eventually stand in front of me with cute smiles on their faces then fold their arms sticking them across their ribs to bunch up their little breasts. We all couldn't help but break out into laughter at this ploy; they are actually trying to impress upon me that they are young eligible women. I take a couple of photos and they make signs that they would like to have copies so I will get Don to do me some prints and I'll return to the island with them later.

We wander about buying some freshly caught fish for about the equivalent of 25p each then look around a little hotel they have on the island, *The Arnulfo*. It is really no more than a king-size bamboo hut but with proper beds and a bar. I get a small lad to find me the little girls after he had taken a look at their photographs; when he returns with them I give separate photos and a pair of earrings to each then I give them both a little peck on the cheek and climb into the dinghy to leave. As we are preparing to go they both cry and try to climb in to go with me. They are still crying as I depart; I should think they're only about twelve years old.

It is very hard to accept that if the islands are ever affected by global warming most of these lovely people will be wiped out as the islands are only about a foot above the high water level.

We have a bit of rain overnight and at daybreak the sky is overcast; the mainland is really close now and we can see the mighty Andes standing high out of the low lying mist. It is a beautiful and somewhat mysterious sight. At the next group of islands the largest one is named Sidra or The Double One. More children wanting their photographs taken soon visit us; we even get a visit from four gorgeous teenage girls accompanied by their mother. We invite the girls on board and give them an ice-cold coke to drink but when we offer to show them round the boat their mother makes them stay in the cockpit. The visit lasts for about thirty minutes and never once during that time do they stop giggling.

Later we set sail to one of the last islands in the whole San

Blas group, Porvanir. This island is very different from the rest having a landing strip for the daily plane and two average-sized hotels. We buy six crabs and six lobsters for $2 which we boil; they provide a hearty, tasty dinner well washed down with G and Ts.

Heavy rain during the night means that all hatches have had to be closed. We need to call at the customs office to pay a fee for cruising in the San Blas; $10 a boat is not bad for the great time we've had here.

The first faulty alternator has to be replaced so I get down to it and get the charging system working again; what an awkward job it is and very hot work too. I think it's time to cut my hair short and shave off my beard.

The batteries are low so we start the auxiliary generator but it stops working after a few minutes; Fatman takes it apart and finds it has a four-stroke engine and he has mixed oil into the fuel. "Ah, well..."

There are lots of reefs around where the local fishermen dive for lobsters; our crews have a go but aren't very successful. After we've explored the island Trev's wife Carole calls him on his satellite phone to give him a new call sign for his EPIRB emergency beacon and also to inform him that an extension to my travel insurance has come through. Finally she adds that 60mph gales are battering England while we here are basking in bright sunshine kept at a steady 26 degrees Celsius by a pleasant breeze.

We go over in the RIB to Wichubhuala, another nearby island, where I buy a genuine handmade panama hat for $5. I drink a glassful of kava made from tree roots and fermented by young girls spitting into it. It is said to be an aphrodisiac and I give the curious girls a demonstration of the instant potency of the legendry brew. I also buy a pretty bead bracelet for my granddaughter Jessica. For dinner we eat five more lobsters between us; after dinner it's time to weigh anchor and wave our goodbyes to Wichubhuala before sailing off to Uchutupu Pippi and Uchutupu Dumat.

These islands are completely surrounded by a coral reef with only a 20ft wide gap to pass through. Dumat is inhabited by very friendly Indians and we are allowed to look around their village watching as they bake bread inside an old forty-five gallon oil drum heated by wood and coconut shells. Some of the crew attempt snorkelling. I too try my hand but just can't get the hang of it. I keep ending up with a mask full of water so I admit defeat and call it a day.

For lunch we finish off the last of the crabs. There isn't a lot of meat on them but then I am only used to crabs caught off the English coast. During the afternoon we bathe luxuriously in the very warm, clear waters of the sea. Trev and Coral go off on their own for a walk so when I get an invitation from Ady to join them on *Da Capo* for drinks I immediately accept. Of course I finish up with a skinful again.

Trev finds his glasses in the dinghy, broken of course. We repair them with cotton and glue after which both crews go to a tiny island near the passé in the reef for another swim and more snorkelling. I am finding it good this time although it takes me a while to get used to the breathing.

After sampling a few cans I accompany Sue for a walk around Dumat; we are wading at the water's edge when I see an octopus near to some rocks; I grasp it by the head to throw it onto the beach but it reacts by snatching my arm and squirting ink at me. An Indian youth seeing my plight comes to my aid, grabs it by a tentacle and beats its head on a rock until it is dead. He guts and cleans it and when that is done sells it to me for 1$; the fee for fishing in his pond.

At around 1900 hours, as we sit eating octopus tentacles dipped in garlic and curry sauce, a squall approaches bringing a downpour.

At 1000 hours the following day we leave the San Blas islands and their inhabitants (some of the nicest people I have ever met) behind.

Chapter 5

Panama

We experience a beautiful sail during the forty-five miles to the Isla Grande pushed along by a twenty knot wind and apart from one very brief downpour we have sunshine all the way. The entry into the anchorage appears to be dangerously narrow but on nearing it we find that it is a lot wider than it had first appeared. We are now very close to the Panamanian mainland and it is a really impressive sight with its high, jungle-covered mountains.

Once ashore we stay close together as we had been warned to take care. We keep our eyes peeled for any signs of trouble but thankfully there are none.

Calling in a bar for a rum and coke we quickly leave when there is an attempt to rip us off. The bar owner goes out to the local shop for a cheap bottle then tries to sell it to us at a pound a shot. Little does he realise he has missed a good opportunity to make a fair amount of honest cash out of us.

Further on we find a Chinese-owned bar and here we are treated fairly so we stay for the whole evening. We eat Chinese meals costing only about the equivalent of £2 each and drink rum at £8.75 a litre.

My shipmates tell me that I fell off the jetty into the dinghy on the way back but luckily I only landed on my head.

Back on the boat Coral sets about Fatman because she's caught him out. He waited until everyone went to bed and then began swilling down the bottles of wine that the rest of us have shared the cost of. At the time of purchase he had actually complained about his contribution until we reduced his share of the cost to stop his moaning.

'It's only right because...' he'd said at the time, 'I am a very light drinker.'

I have already caught him out earlier and asked the others to stay awake to bear witness and this Coral has done, catching him in the act.

Shopping for eggs the next morning I find them so scarce that I take back two bottles of rum instead. 'Well, I think rum is a fair substitute for a breakfast fry-up, don't you?' I defend myself to my hungry mates.

In view of my new-found confidence I decide to buy myself a snorkel and mask at a local diving school where the guy in charge says it will cost US$35, but when he delivers it he has upped the price to $50 so I quickly tell him where he can shove it. I also tell him it will hurt.

Taking a trip ashore in the dinghy to the local supermarket we again find very inflated prices so buy only essentials before setting off on our passage to Portobello. It is a pity that the Isla Grande local traders are so greedy as it is such a lovely place.

When we reach Portobello it really is a beautiful sight with its long bay surrounded by very high hills and we begin to appreciate why Columbus named it so. Portobello translates as Port of Beauty.

The town became famous as the place to where all the stolen gold was taken by the Spaniards for storage awaiting transportation to Spain. They would rob and pillage in Chile, and what is now Ecuador, then carry the loot over the Andes. Sometimes there was so much gold that it wouldn't fit into the storerooms and had to be stacked in the streets. It was also the place where English privateers waited to raid the treasure ships; and what a place for an ambush.

About three miles from the town the entrance to the bay is a bottleneck where most of the battles took place. Just beyond the bay is Drake's Island where, it is said, the body of Sir Francis Drake is buried. We sail into the bay anchoring close to the old fortifications, which we later explore.

Taking the dinghy we set off for the town to discover on arrival that there is no jetty as such, but luck is with us as by mistake we tie up to a private jetty. The owner beckons us to enter the town via his house and he warns us that there are four bars in town but we would be fortunate to leave alive if we were to venture into any of them.

'Furthermore,' he adds, 'for the past few days you have put yourselves in great danger; you are in the province of Colon, one of the most feared places in South America.'

We don't stay long after receiving that information, just long enough to take a tour around the fortifications, which we find to be both fascinating and well preserved.

The villains of the town are, as villains usually are, bone idle and would never dream of climbing hills even to carry out villainy. Once again we have to continue with only essential supplies. We move up the bay for the night, anchoring well out of view from the town. We are entertained continuously by howler monkeys in the surrounding jungle and what a racket they make. It's like listening to a colony of wailing banshees.

At only fifteen miles off Panama we arise early to get off to a flying start. There is a steady breeze and the sun is shining. The windlass stops working; I have to pull up the anchor and fifty metres of chain by hand after which I am knackered. It takes eight cans of ice-cold beer before I am fully recovered.

Our trip is good and passes quickly; soon we are inside the anchorage waiting our turn to pass through the canal. There are massive ships all around and constant action. We find the best thing to do is anchor well out of the way of larger vessels that are on the move.

In the afternoon both *Antinea* and *Da Capo* crews visit the Panama Canal Yacht Club and between us drink several large jugs of ale. The Yacht Club is a really pleasant place; drinks and meals are in the main cheap, but the price of a gin and tonic is a joke. Apparently even though gin is cheap and plentiful tonic water is a scarce and expensive commodity. By the end of the night we find ourselves drinking almost neat gin.

In the pilot we are informed that to leave the security compound and go to San Christobal would be tantamount to committing suicide.

'You would be entering an urban jungle where taxis are plentiful but so are knives and guns. You would almost certainly be robbed or killed; there is little respect for human life.'

So we all keep a low profile and stay inside the compound. We eat dinner at the yacht club tonight followed by downing G and Ts back on the boat.

Come morning we are asked to move the boat but

unfortunately the windlass gives up completely and we have to manhandle the anchor again. A surveyor comes on board to take all our particulars; he measures the boat and tells us to wait for a slot and be prepared as we could then be ordered through at a moment's notice. A toll of $500 to travel the eighty miles through to the Pacific has to be paid and we must keep up a speed of 7 knots.

We meet with the agent handling our passage and he takes the windlass for repair; the end housing has broken. One thing you find in South America is that nothing happens unless bribes are paid; this is why it is necessary to use the agent. He pays the bribes and the authorities make certain that nothing moves unless it is done through him.

The heat here is almost unbearable but the mosquitoes are fewer than usual. We have one small setback; by not being on mains power we haven't got the use of our air conditioning so the number of cold cans that we empty rises dramatically.

I use Trev's satellite phone to contact my daughter-in-law, Tracey, for the first time since I left England. It is great to speak to her and my granddaughter Jessica. Tracey tells me they have got their new house and should be in it by end of the month.

Sue, Don, Fatman and Marvin take a taxi to Panama City on the Pacific Coast a hundred miles away. Tony, Lucy's dad, is to join *Da Capo* tonight and my thoughts are that he may be in for quite an eye opener when he arrives.

I've been suffering with a cold for a couple of days. Can you imagine that in the weather we are enjoying? Anyway I go into my first aid kit for some of my cold cures and find that *Marvin* has used every one. I give him Scarborough warning.

It is the evening of 3rd February and the two crews have dinner in the Yacht Club; the agent has left a message saying that we may be leaving on Friday the 8th. The news gives us plenty to talk about and the discussions are continued back on the boat; naturally over more G & Ts.

Morning dawns and after breakfast Fatman and Marvin inflate the spare dinghy and I check and clean the spark plug; the engine starts almost at once and it hasn't been used for months. Trev and Coral go into the free zone to stock us up with supplies for the next leg. Ady has good news; a new electronics board has arrived so he soon has his auto-helm working again.

Tony pays a call on us after breakfast. The last time I saw him was in the swimming pool at Ady's home. We sign in at the local immigration office before calling in at the Yacht Club for an afternoon session while we are ashore.

Once again we are having trouble with the batteries not holding the charge and ask the agent to get someone to look into it for us. The electrician arrives to check the charging system as evening falls but we run out of diesel and have to borrow some from Ady before we can be up and running again. All goes well until the Fatman starts gobbing off again telling the electrician how to do the job, so the guy walks off the boat and we are never to set eyes on him again. We all dine out together at the Yacht Club then Trev, Coral and I end the day back on *Antinea* sharing a bottle of champagne.

It's Saturday and I collect some very large batteries from *Da Capo* and install them to *Antinea* motors after which everybody lazes about for the rest of the day, eating snacks and drinking champagne until we are blathered.

"It's time to find myself a female companion," I decide and place an advert on the Yacht Club notice board. A couple of days later I check the board for responses without result.

Spending another lazy day my thoughts are inspired to try advertising for a lady companion on the club notice board one more time, only this time I will re-word my plea to hopefully sell myself better, describing myself as an "eligible young man."

Tuesday evening it is dinner at the club again after which we return to *Da Capo* in the dinghies ending the night getting soaked in water fights by throwing buckets of sea water at each other from dinghy to dinghy and getting sozzled drunk on gin.

It's Wednesday and we order a taxi to take us to Panama City; en route we have to pass through San Christobal and I can then well believe all the warnings we've been given.

Seeing the way the people live is beyond belief; they are like rats in holes. In the Hispanic part of town the homes are of acceptable appearance but the African section is a dire slum. Here men and women lie out in the trash-piled streets; most of the flats are windowless and have no doors fitted - just gaps where they've been. I wonder if they have used the doors for firewood. The area really is the pits.

Our ride across to the West Coast is great costing us $20 each; our driver David can speak good English and is a great asset to us. On our arrival in Panama City we are surprised when he introduces us to two armed policemen who agree to escort us around during our stay. The cops tell us to keep bunched together otherwise we will be robbed even though they are very close to us. We walk around with one cop in front and one behind. Every time we have to cross a road they halt the traffic for us; it feels akin to being royalty. They lead us to any shop that we want to visit, entering the store ahead of us and ensuring that the staff give each one of us priority over the other customers. A big bonus is that they also arrange for us to receive a discount on all our purchases.

When we are about ready to return to the boat we take the cops for a snack at a Burger King and give them $10 each; their response is a look that seems to say 'you tight sods' but still they smile and wave as we leave.

On our return we have G and Ts at the Yacht Club followed by champagne on the *Antinea*; Ady joins us for a short while before leaving in a foul mood telling us,

'I'm going to sort things out on the boat between my bloody disgruntled crew.'

On Thursday both crews go ashore to play boules and frisbee on spare ground beside the marina and while we are there we find a pontoon berth; it is a much better place to moor the boat.

At the club that evening Ady tells me that he has given Tony the "hard word", telling him he should either turn a blind eye to the relationship between him and his daughter or get off the boat.

The same evening Fatman puts another nail in his own coffin. You see, every time we go for a night out we always leave a tip. It has been noticed that Fatman always organises the collection of our money and the payment of the final bill but we are now about to find out what he's been up to.

There is a very nice local woman known as 'Amazing Grace' who waits on us every time we go in the yacht club; in gratitude for her good service we always include enough money when settling up for her to get a tip. Tonight is no exception so we are really surprised when she comes into the bar to ask us for more money saying she's been underpaid. On sorting the problem out with her we tumble to his little game. Fatman has been taking our share of the bill and tips from us then adding only enough of his own cash to just cover the actual bill; he's been on the make for weeks. However he's slipped up badly tonight and we tell him so in no uncertain terms.

After leaving the club I help with a crew change on to a nearby tug by using our RIB. One of the men tells me that only a few weeks earlier a gang of bandits came into the marina in speed boats. They tried to shoot up the place but guards and several boat owners retaliated with gunfire and the bandits fled. He says it was pure luck that no one was killed. We also hear about a festival held earlier that day in Panama City when fifteen people were killed during the parade due to an outbreak of violent behaviour.

As we are due to leave tomorrow morning I check everything on the boat. We had to hire some fenders at a cost of $10 each and find they are only old tyres enclosed in plastic bin bags. I also refit the windlass which has been returned ready for the trip while Trev goes off to buy several crates of spirits to build up our stocks.

Tasks done I go to meet a thirty-five-year-old woman from Belgium called Kazzer who has answered my advert for a companion. She is after a lift to the French Polynesian Islands and agrees at once to join us even though I make it clear that she will have to share my bed.

We are due to leave at 0430 hours in the morning so together we stow all our gear including the two inflatables. I have invited Kazzer to join me in the Yacht Club for dinner; Fatman takes over and monopolises all conversation with her. This is typical of him and I get more and more rattled; when the others leave I think,

"Now it is time for me to kick him out." Before I get the

opportunity the cheeky sod says to me,

'Isn't it time for bed, Arthur?' I answer his question bluntly. 'It certainly is, so piss off and leave me to it.'

Kazzer and I are then able have a chat alone before leaving for an early-to-bed night together.

Everyone is up at 0300 hours and after a light breakfast we are soon on our way to the collecting area and motoring around until 0500 hours when two pilots join us; they stay with us until we are through to the other side.

Kazzer, who is a pleasant woman, has been back and forth through the canal several times and is a real asset on the trip. She knows everything there is to be done as she and I work together. She's a hefty lass so I let her haul the large warps in while I sit back and take up the slack. *Antinea* has to be raised 85ft through three massive locks along with a very large cargo ship. She is rafted to two other yachts and we have to brace ourselves every time the ship moves on as there is always one hell of a back wash from the prop. The water-maker bursts another pipe but there is nothing I can do until we are through the canal.

Trev takes me to one side and tells me, 'we might have a bit of a problem, Arthur.'

Bastard Fatman has been to him to complain about Kazzer and me. He told Trev it was really him that she liked and what I am doing isn't fair. Trev says he explained to him about my advert and why she was here but he still whinged.

I reassure Trev. 'There'll be no problem, I'll have it all sorted before the day is over.'

On our way through we cross a lake set in the middle of dense jungle. The whole canal is very impressive and I find out that when the French were building the canal thousands of workers died from yellow fever until finally work on it was stopped.

The Americans then took the job over; first thing they did was to tackle the mosquito problem using DDT and the insects were almost all wiped out. Their next task was to build a massive dam to block off a valley and at the same time to build the Gatun Lock system. Once work was over the lake was allowed to fill.

Gatun Lake is essential to the operation of the locks as it acts as a reservoir to hold water from the mountains while also acting as a waterway across the isthmus.

We have all on to maintain a speed of 7 knots and the two guys on board are there to make us keep up with the cargo boat. As we are going through the last lock into the Pacific I take Kazzer to one side and tell her what has taken place between Fatman and Trev.

'What a load of crap,' she responds.

Even after such a short acquaintance Kazzer dislikes Fatman intensely. I explain that she can stay but I am surely going to give him a bloody good hiding if she does and this might upset Trev; she agrees that it may be for the best if she leaves. Luckily there is an Australian boat rafted to us and we chatted to the owner on the way over. She has a word with him then gets her kit together and shouts out to me,

'See you mate.' I look up, wave and catch my last glimpse of her stepping aboard the Aussie boat.

"Here today, gone tomorrow," is my only thought as I carry on with my chores.

Trev asks me what the hell has happened, and when I tell him his belated advice is:

'Silly bugger, you should have kept her and flattened him.'

My first sighting of the Pacific is as we approach the Americas Bridge. It is a great sight and the start of what I really came on this trip for.

We pick up a mooring in the bay and sort the necessary jobs out before heading into town for a good night out. It's a good night apart from the crap food we get served up in a restaurant. It is so bad that we argue until we get the bill reduced.

I don't usually bear a grudge but now Fatman is really in my bad books. I take him on one side and warn him that from now on he had better keep his nose out of my affairs or face the consequences.

Next day I grab a taxi into town in search of a store that sells high pressure hose suitable for the water-maker; I am sold some that is supposed to be the same specification but when fitted it only lasts half an hour. Sitting back to study the unit I come to the conclusion that the pressure control valve has been fitted in the wrong place; it takes me a couple of hours to alter but proves to be well worth the effort as we have less trouble after that.

On another trip into Panama City, that takes about three hours, we buy two very large deep cycle batteries then we shop in a supermarket where our bill comes to $421. This may seem a lot but shared between five it isn't all that much and it will be another two weeks before we get the chance to buy any more. We have a good laugh out of it too; I saw a case of Moet Chandon at $43.64 and showed it to Trev who then threw three cases in a trolley. Before we reach the checkout we discover the price is per bottle so we have to dump that particular trolley load.

I've had a very busy day fitting the batteries. Ady set off to Ecuador but he'd to turn back with diesel in his water tanks as they had to be drained and flushed before he could move on again. The shipping agent comes to get the account settled and clear us through immigration then we are ready for off at 0630 hours the next morning.

Just as we are about to cast off Coral drops a pillow case over board; the stupid Fatman dives straight in to retrieve it, just as the lock gates are opened. He suddenly finds himself being washed out to sea in a four-knot current. Marvin immediately begins running round like a headless chicken shouting,

'Where's the fuel can? Get the dinghy paddles.' Plus many more stupid comments.

By this time I have tied a series of warps onto the dinghy while Coral lets them out until it is close enough for Fatman to grab. He hangs on to the dinghy as we haul him back aboard.

'I hope that there's somebody other than Marvin around if ever I fall overboard,' I tell Coral.

Off we go to the Las Pearlas Islands where it is reputed natives still hunt with bows and arrows. The water-maker is now working well and the batteries seem to be holding charge although we have turned the freezer off to be on the safe side.

When we reach the Isla Contra Dora it is Coral's fiftieth

birthday and we go ashore to celebrate, meeting up with the *Da Capo* bunch in a bar. We all drink iced Sangria until we get fresh and then take a walk around the island. Later we play frisbee on a beach that has the best sand I've ever seen; it is as fine as flour and almost pure white.

Isla Contra Dora is mainly inhabited by wealthy Panamanians and used for entertaining visiting foreign politicians; it has tarmac roads and even sleeping policemen.

A party on *Da Capo* later in the evening results, as our parties so often do, in everyone getting absolutely blotto.

The new day is full of promise and my expectation of a good time is high; after breakfast we sail about five miles to Isla Casaya. The weather and sea state are still beyond belief. We anchor in ten metres and I go off to the beach. I never see any live shellfish but I do see scallop shells that are nine inches across and one cockle shell measuring about six inches across.

I take a stroll and find a large rock pool full of fish and sea cucumbers where I spend some time swimming in the warm water alongside the marine life.

During our stay a native visits us in his dugout canoe and sits holding onto our boat for about half an hour without ever saying a word. We offer him ice-cold beer which he seems to like then he just smiles and leaves without either a thank you or a kiss my arse.

The natives on Isla Casaya have pigs running loose on the beach and in the jungle. They also have a large boar tied up like a guard dog on a chain outside a shack which takes an instant dislike to Trev, snapping at his legs when he tries to walk close to it. After a barbecue dinner on the boat I only drink a small amount of wine before turning in for an early night.

It's morning again and we sail off to Isla Viveros in what is another perfect sunny day; we have to avoid several dangerous reefs while sailing to the anchorage situated in a large sandy bay.

There are many small islands that are not named on maps and charts so even though we visit and explore as many as possible we frequently cannot put a name to some of them.

On Isla Viveros I wander off on my own finding a secluded spot where I can skinny dip and sunbathe, leaving Fatman and

Marvin to explore some small islands. Later Coral accompanies Trev and me to yet another small island where we collect lots of periwinkles and limpets in a bucket of salt water. We try catching fish from the dinghy on the way back to *Antinea* but are not very successful.

When darkness falls Ady calls me to join him with our dinghy; his own RIB has gone adrift and it can't be seen anywhere. He comes with me and together we motor around for a while without seeing it; we cut the engine to find in which direction we are drifting then go in the same direction as the current, stopping a few times to scan around by torchlight until we see something. It is indeed his lost dinghy; he is really pleased to find it and invites me back to *Da Capo* for a drink.

While I am on *Da Capo* disaster strikes on *Antinea*; she has drifted over a submerged reef and touched down on it.

Trev believes that if Fatman and Marvin had behaved as they should, he could possibly have got off the reef. He told them to get the boom out at right angles to the boat and immediately climb out on it but they both totally ignored him. Instead of obeying his instructions they kept radioing to *Da Capo* for advice.

The opportunity is by now lost and the boat has settled down hard onto the reef and the rudder is also stuck in a cleft. As the boat moves about on the swell severe damage is done to the rudder. I myself have been in a similar situation on another boat and I think Trev is perfectly correct in thinking that the damage could have been avoided by instant action from a more obedient crew.

At 0330 hours we float free but are still unaware of the full extent of the damage. Trev gives both Fatman and Marvin a right proper bollocking telling them that it is about time that they learned to take orders from just one skipper.

Later we set sail for the Isla Del Rey but on the way our auto-helm packs in; I examine it to find the ball joint connecting a quadrant to the ram has sheared off. It is a new break and may have saved the rudder from irreparable damage.

At Del Rey we sail into a bay, calling at a village called Esmeralda. Close to the village there are dozens of small fishing boats and all the natives appear busy. Walking around the village we do a bit of shopping and take photos of the children until I notice a small bar. Trev, Coral and me go in and are enjoying a can of cold beer when Ady enters. He discreetly lets us know to get the hell out of the bar; as we head back to the beach he points to a stack of almost new, very expensive looking outboard motors saying,

'There is no way these people can afford to have paid for them and there is only one other way they can have acquired them.'

We return to the boats and leave the island in a hurry sailing to another bay much further down the coast. Here there is a small manned coastguard station close to the beach and we drop the hook about 300 metres off. Ady takes Lucy ashore but while Trev and me are below decks Fatman and Marvin follow them in our RIB. When he finds out Trev is very angry; we are now stuck on the boat as it would have taken hours to get the spare dinghy unearthed and prepared for use. We also see that they haven't had the sense to pull the dinghy above the water line and the tide is rising. Luckily the two coastguards notice their error and drag the dinghy up the beach to safety.

Ady and Lucy are furious when they get back; they had obviously gone ashore to have a bit of privacy and now they too have taken a dislike to Fatman and Marvin. The Girls, as we also at times refer to Fatman and Marvin, collectively, are fast making enemies.

When we get back the use of our dinghy Trev, Coral and me go to the coastguard station to have a chat with the two young lads there. They are from Panama and do regular two-week stints. We notice that they are well-armed and have a large radio set inside their shack.

During our chat with them we mention to the coastguards that we intend to go further up the coast to explore a river there but they advise us that bandits are in the area and it would be a good idea to stay well clear.

We take a walk up the nearby path and along a large air force runway to the other side of the island. There is little left of the old barracks and most of the roads have become overgrown but the runway is still in a good state and it would be an ideal place for transferring illegal goods if one was so minded.

On our way back one of the lads (the guards) passes us brandishing a machine gun. He doesn't speak but just walks around the runway where we have just been. Back at the beach we are asked to give details of our boat and crew.

Fatman and Marvin had told Trev that when they sneaked off with the dinghy to Isla Del Rey they discovered a little reservoir created by the guards who had built a dam to form it. This gave them somewhere to bathe and do washing of pots or anything else they needed to clean. Trev now takes us to the reservoir. He gives us a demonstration of how the wooden bung in the dam, that they use as a tap, works. Suddenly the one piece bung is now two pieces. In his words,

'When I was fitting it back in the hole it simply fell apart in my hand.'

We make a temporary repair and skedaddle. While walking back along the beach we find ten large oysters among the rocks, which we collect to eat later.

I am so worn out when we get back at 1930 hours that I go straight to bed without supper. I am up again at 0730 hours next morning trying to repair the auto-helm but unfortunately we haven't the equipment I need to do it.

A local fishing boat comes alongside and we buy five red snappers from them before a lot of time is spent stowing our gear and preparing for our next journey which will take us to Ecuador. For dinner we have roast beef and Yorkshire pudding followed by a dessert course - a booze-up. Regardless of the booze-up we are all up early this morning and get under way by 0845 hours.

The windlass is playing up a bit and a pipe on the water-maker blows an olive off the end but I easily fix that.

About ten miles out we catch a big tuna. It will make a couple of meals for all of us. It's an ideal day for sailing and we go for miles using the spinnaker. We should really have taken it down about 1800 hours as the wind is increasing but Trev said it would be okay and I go off watch at 1900 hours. About two hours later I am awakened by him screaming for it to be brought down. I run out onto the foredeck shouting for the pole to go forward and down so that I can reach the release shackle. Fatman and Marvin have no idea, they are so slow in sorting out the sheet and up-haul that the sail is torn in two; Marvin hasn't even released the halyard so we have to sail all through the night with half of the sail blowing about at the top of the mast. I go back on watch at 0300 hours and am on the helm until almost 0900 hours then I help to get the torn sail down. During the day we see our first shark; it is very big one and swimming only about twenty metres away.

Sunday 24th February is another good day with plenty of wind even though we are passing through the doldrums. We are sailing with the Genoa poled out together with a full main at a speed of 8 knots and about eighty miles from land. We've checked the spinnaker to find that it will require a specialist repair. Ady reports that he's had a very large dorado on the line but couldn't land it which is a pity as it would have yielded several meals. The two boats are staying close together as we are still in bandit country; in the evening we sail even nearer to *Da Capo* stern to enable them to float a frozen turkey across to us on the end of a line.

As we are unwinding the Genoa the reefing line comes off the drum and gets jammed so badly that I have to cut it loose and then rewind it, all this while sitting in the anchor locker. I have cramp so bad when it is finished that I actually have to crawl back to the cockpit. I eat dinner and drink a few G and Ts then take a short nap. I am out again on watch from 2130 to 0130 hours then settle down for a good night's sleep.

The new day has a cooler start with 19 knots of wind. *Antinea* is sailing on 210 degree while *Da Capo* goes on to 185 although she never sails further than two or three miles ahead.

Trev bakes dried fruit and banana bread which is a very tasty alternative to our diet. On the whole we have a pleasant day seeing two pilot whales jump completely clear of the water; they then follow us for miles keeping us well entertained by their antics.

At this point we are getting low on food but we still manage a tasty meal of egg, spam, and pasta. The wind dies down after

1830 hours but we keep up a speed of 5.5 knots. Overnight we have to motor for six hours and get a bit of rain about 0430 hours but all in all it's been a good twenty-four hours. We are still sailing close together most of the time mainly to deter any would-be pirates.

During the afternoon a tiny bird lands on board and more or less takes over the boat. First of all it flies around landing from time to time on someone, including me. This fun is all very well while it lasts but then it flies into the cabin and begins shitting over everything, charts, food, bedding, in other words it is making a proper nuisance of itself.

Fatman and Marvin lose concentration while playing about with it and let the mainsail gybe. The boom goes through hitting Trev across the forehead and knocking his glasses over the side of thc boat.

"It's time to put an end to this and get on with sailing the boat," I decide, so catching the bird I wring its neck.

It makes me very unpopular for a while but at least no one else gets hurt and the boat is soon back to normal with everyone paying attention to what matters most: safe sailing.

Tonight we cross the Equator and celebrate the event with champagne. Though I get well merry, Fatman, Marvin and Trev really get blathered and I have to take over the helm and am thirty miles further on before anyone else is fit to relieve me. After the initial excitement of crossing the line my thoughts have to be concentrated on the responsible business of sailing the boat whilst the others sleep it off.

I have a rude awakening at 0730 hours, Trev calls me out on deck and tells me to make myself look as big as possible then he indicates behind me. Alongside is a large dugout canoe with the four Indians in it all shouting and waving at us. We decide to ignore them and carry on at full speed but they keep up with us and appear to be getting more aggressive. By now we are getting seriously worried as to what might be the outcome of this incident, occurring while the recent killing of Sir Peter Blake is still fresh in our minds. Suddenly Marvin shouts,

'I think there are some nets alongside.'

We look and sure enough can see a long line of floats;

changing course we motor away as quickly as possible. At once the men in the canoe begin to smile and come alongside, probably with the same relief as us that it is all over. They make signs to us that they would like some cigarettes but having none we offer them cans of beer which they eagerly accept. We all had a good laugh and they leave us to continue on our way. Their nets are to go on for several more miles before we leave them behind but that is nothing of a problem compared to the one if the fishermen had been the bandits we feared they were.

During this incident we have actually been more than forty miles from land and it happens during a tropical storm; but we are so hyped up that no one seems to have noticed the bad weather.

Shortly after this the engine cuts out; I check it out and find the main tanks are empty. Luckily we have an untapped full tank, which was converted to fuel from water by the experts in Curacao. The fitter gave us instructions for changing from one tank to another but when I try it nothing happens. It turns out that he has installed a priming pump at the wrong end of the fuel line. It takes me quite some time to sort it out but eventually I succeed and manage to bleed the system; yet the engine still won't start.

Trev spots water mixed in with the fuel so I remove a large inspection cover from the tank to discover that they didn't even drain the water from the tank during the conversion. I have to siphon as much neat fuel off the surface of the water as possible and pour it into the main tank. Next I clear all the fuel lines, change the filter and pump the water from the injector pipes; the engine starts at once. We are again underway, well, for a short time until the alternator drive belt flies off.

We carry several spares so I soon have a new one fitted, but before much more time elapses I have to replace a burst pipe on the water-maker; it just isn't our day.

Chapter 6

Ecuador

Both boats arrive at Salinas Marina, Ecuador at about 2400 hours; we are met by the local agent, a Canadian named George. We've taken heed of the warnings about Colombian bandits but are unprepared for a Canadian bandit.

Permission is granted to tie up to the fuelling pontoon for the night and to celebrate our arrival we once again all get pissed. I am slightly woozy when I awake the next day to find that our food reserves are almost gone but still manage to scavenge enough food for breakfast.

While Trev and Ady are sorting out immigration I take Coral for a walk. Of course, under my directions we get lost and have to turn back to take another route.

During our walk she opens up a little and begins to tell me of her feelings for me; I, too, become aware of feeling a little affection for her and I ask her to go into the seaside resort of Salinas with me for the afternoon. As we hop into a taxi together I little realise this is going to be the start of something good.

Salinas is a nice place and turns out to have a great beach. We stop at a bar for a few beers before making our way to the supermarket only returning to the boatyard when we've purchased a large supply of food.

On our arrival back at the marina we see the workers are preparing to lift the boat out to begin repairs. *Antinea* has to be moved off the pontoon and the harbour workers give us a hand. It's a good job, too, because we have to moor stern-on to a rocky sea wall, something they are more used to doing than ourselves.

While still in the water I have to pickle the water-maker. This is done to preserve the delicate membrane that filters the water. I am almost finished when Trev returns so together we get the boat ready to be lifted onto the hard-standing.

Come evening both full crews go together into Salinas to a restaurant and have a very nice meal followed by a few drinks. The Ecuadorians appear very friendly and once again, their girls are beautiful. I try to send some e-mails but find my address has been withdrawn due to lack of use. When you visit islands that are off the beaten track loss of contact with the outside world is just one price you must be prepared to pay. There are others, like coping with missing close family and friends.

In Ecuador we find more mosquitoes than we have ever known anywhere before. I have always kept up with my pills and so don't expect any problems.

I've noticed the meter on the water maker is leaking so I by pass it and soon have it in good working order again. It is important as we will soon be leaving on a long tour of the interior, a trip I am really looking forward to.

It is almost dark before the boat is high and dry so as soon as we finish we head to town. Another restaurant is decided upon this time, one at which Trev and Ady ate when they visited immigration earlier. We are served an excellent meal and everything goes well apart from bloody Fatman gobbing off again. He just can't resist trying to belittle everyone. Trev gives him a proper dressing down and everyone else says they are getting fed up of listening to him. After the meal we manage to lose him in town and arriving back at the boat before either him or Marvin we quickly get the wine out to finish off the evening.

When he does return Fatman is as queer as his arse and goes straight to bed. Trev and I down another bottle of wine and go to bed the worse for wear.

Sending all my dirty clothes to the laundry the next day I assume they will be back before we set off on our trip to the hinterland, but no; I end up with only three shirts to take on the trip.

Trev has a row with the double act Fatman and Marvin before we leave. He needs two extra fenders to hang over the boat sides but they tell him they have lost two overboard at separate times previously when they were on watch.

Trev asks, 'Why didn't you tell me at the time?' and they answer,

'You were asleep when it happened and we thought that to go looking for them was a waste of time.'

Replacements cost $100 each so it would certainly have

been very productive to recover them.

They also tell him that they were busy when it happened as they had run into some nets and had to cut the boat free. Now if they had told him this at the time he would have had a watch on the bow looking for more. It would have saved a lot of anxiety when we were chased by the fishermen.

March 2nd and we leave for a self-organised tour of Ecuador taking two taxis to Guayacil, a seaport about seventy-five miles away. I am to hear later it has the reputation of being one of the two most dangerous ports in the world. This day is also to be the last time we ever set eyes on Fatman and Marvin.

The journey takes us through some interesting areas; there is a lot of very hilly moor land that's badly eroded, as though many flash floods have occurred here. Large villages we pass through appear to be no-go areas, even in broad daylight.

Finally we reach our destination where we visit a travel agency run by a Canadian lady. She warns us about walking around the city, even sending an employee to escort us when we go out for lunch. Through her we book lodgings for the night and two air flights, one from Guayacil to Quito and the other back from Cuenca. The hostel we stay in is a big disappointment, very cheap but even so not worth the amount we've paid. After an almost sleepless night I wake up with at least forty mosquito bites around my midriff. The place is not unlike a Victorian doss house, I hope the rest of our bookings are of better standard than this one.

Earlier we went for dinner to a large restaurant and that was also a big let down. To make matters worse on the way back we were being followed by some very unsavoury examples of humanity and had to make a dash for the safety of our undesirable digs.

The travel agent told us that the Colombians are deeply entrenched in civil war and advised us not to visit the northern parts of Ecuador, an area highly populated by terrorist sympathisers.

I am at this time sharing a room with Tony. We rise early and find a local snack bar for a light breakfast after which we catch the plane to Quito, the capital city. Known as the world's highest capital it is fourteen thousand feet above sea level and this is demonstrated to us during the flight. The flight takes only forty-five minutes and the plane gains height after takeoff but never makes a descent as we approach the airfield; it simply levels and lands. Quito is so high that we need to take things easy for a couple of days until we get used to breathing the thin air.

We find ourselves in the midst of the Andes where we enjoy some very spectacular views throughout our stay in the Hotel Quito, one of the finest here; we only pay $20 for bed and breakfast. It boasts a pool, gardens, and an outside bar and we have an extremely pleasant sojourn.

A visit to the centre of town by taxi brings warnings to "beware" as the inhabitants are amongst the world's best pickpockets. A lot of our time is spent browsing around the busy street markets and we're constantly being warned that we are in a dangerous part of town but I never once feel threatened. I feel secure because there are mostly Indians about and I have always got on well with these people.

We choose a Chinese restaurant for dinner where the waiter advises us that wine we have ordered will cost $28 a bottle but we barter until a final price of $20 is agreed. The meal is excellent but when the bill arrives the wine is priced at $28 and naturally we refuse to pay. The staff argue for a while until Ady puts the money on a table and tells them that they have a choice.

'Take what's offered or I will ask him to clear a way through you to the door.' He means me!

I am pleased to say that his bluff works and we leave without further ado.

Back at the hotel Trev has a bottle of brandy sent to his room and invites me to share it. The brandy goes down a treat but the bill doesn't. When Trev pays the final account he finds that he's been charged $79 for the one bottle. They have actually charged him as though it has been sold in single measures through the optics, plus room service.

Things that have been going through my head for a long time finally surface when Trev brings up the subject by saying:

'I think that The Girls should be off the boat.'

He means Fatman and Marvin.

He's tallied the things lost and broken through their incompetence into monetary terms exceeding a thousand pounds, and then adds,

'That's without counting the nights out we've had ruined whenever Fatman's been around.'

I have a brilliant sleep that night even though the bites I've suffered still itch like crazy. I'm starting to feel great.

The weather is much cooler here but we still only need light clothing. I am amazed at breakfast time when I eat like a horse, having been off my food for most of the trip. I've got to thinking it can only be due to the heat.

Today, our second on this trip, we visit the local cultural centre where we see many interesting Inca artefacts; during the conducted tour I learn a lot about the Inca way of life.

We take another trip to the town and are again warned that we may be putting our lives in danger. While we are there we observe a strong police presence; all are armed and wear riot gear. Rumour is that much government business will be taking place during the course of the day. A reliable source informs us that those running the country are corrupt, ruling through fear and subversion. It is a fact that whenever we come up against any type of officialdom we find we can buy our way out by paying bribes.

In a bar on the way back to the hotel we find the prices are almost too good to be true. Two pints of beer and a bottle of water cost only $2. I am tired out when we eventually get back to the hotel and need a long sleep before going out again.

Coral and Tony stay in that night while the rest of us go to an Italian restaurant where the food is superb. For a laugh we all check our pulses and the average bpm is down to 60 per minute due to the high altitude. We drink a lot of wine while planning the next leg of our tour, then the owner comes to our table and gives each of us a couple of drinks "on the house."

Up at 0730 hours to another good start we breakfast then go down to the bus depot. Here we catch a Pullman coach to Otavala, a lovely Indian town in the mountains. The fare for the two and half hour ride is only $2.

Once there we go to see a tourist agent who recommends a very decent hotel charging $12 for B & B. It really is a good hotel and thankfully spotlessly clean. On taking a short walk around town we find it to be a pleasant place. It is very cool, only about 7c even though we are right on the equator. We've booked a tour for the following day and I need to buy myself a 'showerproof' coat so I set about seeking and eventually buying one.

Evening dinner out of the hotel comprising of a starter, main course, one beer, one coffee, and one whiskey, costs less than £5 then it is back to our hotel for the night.

We are all up to a great breakfast at 0715 hours then off to join the tour. Our transport is a four-seater pickup, meaning two people have to sit in the back. Our first stop is for a stroll through the forest to a waterfall; it is very picturesque and we all enjoy it. The tour includes being taken to see weaving done, then on to a pan-pipe maker. He both gives a demo of making pipes and of playing them. A friend then joins him and together they sing traditional songs. I buy a set of pipes from them for my granddaughter Jessica.

On the next leg the tour drives far up into the mountains to a flooded volcano where we take a boat ride around islands in the crater until it is lunchtime. Trev surprises us by opting for roast guinea pig but from the look on his face when it is served I think he regrets his choice. It comes complete with toenails, eyes, and teeth and I am sure I see it wink at him as he takes his first bite.

The tour continues by taking us to see indigenous Indians in their own environment who are being sponsored by the EEC; now I know where our taxes go. We see sandals being made using sinews of aloe vera plants, an old man weaving mats from reeds, and a witch doctor who allows us to see inside the surgery where he keeps his potions.

All the Indians live in bamboo hovels with earth floors where the only furniture consists of a few old metal containers of the type used for biscuits, recycled to serve as seats or tables, and several hammocks.

On the way back we stop at a shop to buy bottles of rum

and lemonade. The owner pours the lemonade into a plastic carrier bag and won't let us take the bottle from his shop. I just stand there gaping in amazement as he fills the carrier bag with the pop.

Another tour is already booked for a two-day pony trek into the Andes. We are driven by jeep to a farm to collect our mounts. I choose a black horse called Lucia and the two of us get on very well together on the trek.

We travel over twenty kilometres and the whole ride is brilliant. I get into the swing of things from the word go. It's great to be back in a saddle even though it's been many years since I last rode a horse; getting our mounts into a gallop is so exciting.

At the halfway stage we stop for coke and crisps while the ponies are left to have a champ at the grass. There's spectacular scenery all around in every direction; to one side a precipice seems to go down into oblivion backed by beautiful valleys and at the other are steep cliffs with overhanging trees.

I let Lucia, the feminine named gelding do his own thing as he has more experience of the mountain tracks; we eventually reach the tiny village of San Cortez Da Mina. We are to stay in a hostel here that is part of a disco; the rest resembles a dungeon. I think we had a good evening meal but because I drank a little too much Johnny Walker before we ate I can't remember.

'Let's give the village an eyeball,' someone suggests.

We call in at a bar for a game of pool with our two guides but under Ecuadorian rules we haven't a hope in hell of winning a game.

The following morning after a sound sleep I'm told that Coral has been hitting the bottle and ran amok during the night. Trev is furious with her and I don't think he will ever let her forget it.

Our day starts very early to the sound of loud pop music being played in the church next door. We have breakfast before going to the farm where the horses were stabled overnight. I climb on Lucia and ride him bareback to the hostel to saddle up. We're off on our trek again before 0930 hours returning to the farm by a different route.

We see signs of an overnight deluge with debris everywhere and a lot of the track has been washed away. After riding for about four hours we arrive back at our starting point; the horses put on a good show by entering the farmyard at full gallop. It has been a trip I will remember for a long time.

Everyone books back into the same hotel and after dining out I end the day drinking rum and brandy with Trev and Coral.

Saturday March 8th we take a walk down to the local animal sale. There are many species of farm livestock on offer but most animals look half-starved. After leaving the sale we take a bus to Quito and another on to Banyos. I thought the mountains were high in Otavala but they were only pimples in comparison to the ones here. There is an active volcano too, Turangahua; it is very high, overshadowing the small town. As the bus descends into the town of Banyos we are thrown about all over the place as the driver takes action to avoid the many rock slides always in progress. It's a tiny town with everyone living on the edge as the volcano could erupt at anytime. They even have a civilian action force ready to organise evacuation if and when it should happen. I think at first that it may be a bit dodgy to stay here but the more I see of it the more I come to like the place.

On our first night in Banyos we have a meal in what appears to be a very decent restaurant but when I pay a call of nature I am absolutely shocked. The facility provided is disgusting; human excrement is everywhere and you need to wipe your feet on the way out. There is a hole in the floor directly over the stoves where the food is being cooked, but this discovery comes too late for us, we have already eaten. Nevertheless I report my findings to the others and we flee the place pronto.

We view a $3 B and B hostel but the rooms leave a lot to be desired; the one we opt for is a bit more up-market and a notice in the room states that if you find a friend you are allowed to take her back to your room for a small extra charge.

It seems that there is a rift developing between us and the *Da Capo* crew; Trev leads us in different directions on several occasions but I don't let him influence my own relationship with any of them.

In one bar I sample an oddly named drink called a Kamikaze; in no time at all there are lots of dead mosquitoes floating in it. I guess this to be the reasoning behind why the drink is so named.

It is a very noisy night in the hotel so we decide to move on; when we pay our bill I am charged $11 more than I was told it would be when we booked in; if it was assumed I'd taken a friend back then I've missed out somehow. We move to another place charging $8 all-in and that includes doing our laundry.

While paying a visit to a cyber café Trev pulls me to one side and informs me,

'Brace yourself, Arthur; I've just received a bit of bad news. Fatman and Marvin have jumped ship. What are we going to do about it?'

The decision to go to a bar and celebrate is unanimous.

Visiting some hot springs at the base of the volcano we hit a snag: there is a river blocking our way. A bit of rock hopping is necessary to get across and in the process Coral ends up with a very wet backside. When we do get there the place is disappointing as the facilities are filthy and quite unhygienic. Not to be put out we stroll back into town where we book a couple of tours before going out for dinner and then finish the day partying in Trev's room. I wake up next day in Trev's bed and he has ended up in mine so it must have been a good night. I come off best though as Coral is in bed with me; I have at last broken new ground with our lady crew member.

We are having a real change today: white water rafting. A pick up takes us up into the mountains where we are to start the trip. Our first half hour is spent with the raft on the river bank practising rowing and safety procedures. The instructors then tell us we are competent and the raft is dropped into the river. We practise again with the raft tied up but while we are preoccupied they cast us off; we are under way.

Wow, what an experience! We fairly romp along. There are rapids and shallow waterfalls along the route, which we are soon taking in our stride. The idea is to sit right on the outer rim of the raft in order to have better control of the paddles while the lad on the helm shouts when to row, stop, or back paddle. Water in the river is so rough that at times we are almost submerged but it is a fantastic two and half hours.

We have to leave the river at a place where it is about to descend seventy feet while passing through a three-mile long chasm; it is obviously considered too dangerous to raft the river here. We enjoy it so much that we are already planning another trip as we are taken back down the mountains in the pick-up.

I send an e-mail to Virginia who is a friend in Boston, America; I met her in the Azores when on a voyage crossing the Atlantic. Off we then go to a purpose built hot spring spa just up the road from our hostel. Terrific; the water is so hot that I think it could be unbearable but it feels so good I find it difficult to get out. On leaving the hot pool there is a very cold pool to jump into and this is really the icing on the cake. We all feel so good after the experience that we return twice more before leaving Banyos.

The evening descends and we have a good curry meal at a well-run local bistró owned by a Swiss couple before returning to the hostel to do justice to a bottle of wine. While we are enjoying the wine Trev's wife and daughter ring from England and tell him that they would like to come out for a holiday.

After a very early breakfast we are once again off on our travels and for most of the way the bus rides along narrow roads flanked by a 1000ft drop; it's quite scary at times. After rounding one hairpin bend we find the road blocked by oncoming vehicles; the driver has to reverse back around the bend then carry on a long way until there is room to pass.

When we finally reach our destination after about two hours, our guide takes us to a market to buy supplies; shopping is followed by another ride, this time by jeep into the jungle. We stow our gear in a camp before taking off on a trek. We see many types of unusual plants including the fertility tree, which bears shoots that the Indian girls are reputed to use as sex toys. This trek is another experience that I've never in my life expected to have. Making our way through the dense vegetation we come to a cliff with a very high waterfall running down and an inviting pool at its foot. We are all so hot that we strip off and wade in; our guide suggests that we should stand under the fall which of course we do. It is wonderfully exhilarating.

Coral takes her turn under the water and the guide advises her to stand with her arms raised to protect her head but I think his real reason is to get a better view of her breasts as she always goes topless when in water. We dress without bothering to dry because it has started raining and the downpour looks as if it will continue through the night.

It's a long plod through mud back to camp and when eventually we arrive it is well past beer o'clock so we break open the rum and whiskey; our guide ends up really well-oiled. A lady at the camp cooks our chicken making us a good, satisfying meal then we carry on with our little party until very late before going off to bed in the bamboo hut. We have mosquito nets that work a treat. I never get a single bite but we do get stung; someone in the camp steals our remaining bottles of rum and whiskey that we've put aside for the remainder of the trip.

Our guide calls round with bleary eyes the next morning; he seems quite put out when he finds us downing a hearty meal but he gets over his bad start as the day wears on. A walk to a river ensues; here two Indians wait to convey us in a dugout canoe across the fast flowing water to their village. We are shown snakes whose venom is milked for use in medicines; we also see how they make and bake their own pottery. I am even allowed to have a go with a blowpipe and I actually become a bit of a marksman with it. The next stage of our safari is to be the only time in the last six months that I have felt so uneasy.

We are in the dugout again but with only one Indian and are taken downriver; by now the water is a raging torrent and there are only about three inches of freeboard on the canoe. Every time the lad uses the paddle our canoe rocks, taking in water, and we know that the river is home to alligators; I feel very apprehensive. I needn't have worried though as we land safely on the bank; we have no option as it happens because we are close to a big waterfall.

It is time for another walk; arriving at a large camp we are made very welcome by an Indian family we are to stay with. We are shown our sleeping quarters, a bamboo hut on stilts with a ladder up to it. When we reach the kitchen our dinner is already being prepared and Trev tells me to expect a highly-flavoured stew as he has been watching the youth preparing it. He's seen him peel the vegetables and drop them into the pan without bothering to even rinse them. Still the stew goes down well followed by several cans of ale that they keep in a very old fridge.

Heavy rain is still falling so we sit in the kitchen chatting and killing cans. The rest of the family arrive all carrying umbrellas made from banana tree leaves. The old man and his wife are followed by two stunning daughters; we saw them earlier as we walked to the camp, they were picking fruit in the jungle.

'Forget the rain and come to see the girls playing,' the guide tells us.

Outside is a rope hanging from a large tree over the river; they have both changed into something similar to Western style hot-pants and are swinging way out over the muddy water and dropping off the rope. They are unconcerned that the river is by now a sweeping torrent or that alligators lurk in it. When they are through Trev and I award them ten out of ten for the best wet T-shirt display we've seen in a long time.

Later we are taken across the river in a very large canoe by two lads but this time I feel totally safe. We take a walk up on to a plateau where there is a fairly big settlement. At this village they even have a full-size football pitch; everyone here is wearing Wellington boots, which our guide tells us are the best thing to ever come to the jungle. Not only do they keep the feet dry but they are also protection against snakes and scorpions.

When the sun goes down we walk to a large lagoon and by shining our torches are able to pick out the eyes of the many alligators; it is eerie. The rest of the evening is spent eating and drinking beer.

The eldest daughter stays with us to serve the beer, all the time keeping herself amused with a toy her father has made; it is carved in the form of a well-endowed Indian.

The more we drink the more beautiful she appears and soon

we are both making remarks about her anatomy and what we could do with it. She stands there innocent-like with a bemused smile on her face. As we are drinking our last cans she leaves to go to bed and while climbing the ladder to her loft she looks across and with a beaming face says in very good English,

'I hope you enjoyed your evening, gentlemen.'

Trev and I nearly fall off the bench laughing; she has been listening to us all night and knew exactly what we were saying. It wasn't a bemused smile on her face after all, well maybe?

Another hard walk awaits us next day after breakfast; it is up hill all the way and the tracks are slippery with mud; our exertions mean we are very hot when we emerge into the open at the top of the hill. It's been a very hard climb indeed but when we see the view we appreciate it's been well worth it. We see the Rios Puyo and Pastavah where they link up at a massive flood plane before joining the mighty Amazon further downriver. After walking back to camp we down a couple of beers to cool off before packing our bags and leaving to meet the jeep that will return us to civilisation.

Back in Porvanir the guide takes us to a liquor store where we purchase ten bottles of rum at $2.5 each. Then back on board the bus and we are once again riding the dodgy road over the mountain. Most rock falls are simply pushed over the edge of the road but in one place stands a policeman controlling traffic between rock falls. He stops the vehicles if he sees any rocks falling and then waves them on when there is a pause in the avalanche of rocks.

Bus drivers on the route race each other down the mountain roads in order to be first along the way to be able to pick up any would-be passengers.

We are safely back in Banyos and book into a different hostel, the Plantas Y Blanco on the recommendation of George, our last guide. It is a nice place, having a large patio on the roof and a help-yourself-café where you can cook your own food using their equipment.

We meet up with Ady and once again we all go out together for dinner and drinks; a good time is had by all.

I am up at 0630 hours the next morning and sit out on the

patio. An hour later Trev joins me for breakfast then off we go with *Da Capo's* crew to have another bash at rafting. The river level has risen and it is a much faster ride than before. Tony and Ady drop their paddles overboard but they are quickly recovered. Suddenly we strike a rock and Ady is thrown over the front of the raft. He lies on his back with his feet forward as we have been instructed and within a few minutes we've caught up with him and a text book rescue follows. I am very relieved when he is back on board the raft with no obvious injuries.

Due to the recent rain causing the river to run high the rapids are much more fearsome. I suppose that due to our previous experience we are not afraid and have a brilliant time.

Trev says that his wife and daughter are due to arrive in a few days and he will have to leave the group to meet with and entertain them; he will also be leaving Coral in my more than capable hands.

When I awake the next day Trev has already left for Quito. His departure means we have to get taxis to the coach depot to set off on the next leg of our tour, to Riobamba some distance away. We find riding on local transport good; it enables us to get in among the villages and see at first hand how the people live.

They are very poor and life is truly basic but you can instantly notice the sense of pride they feel. The females make the effort to dress smartly and every one has a smile or a nod for us.

Riobamba doesn't turn out to be as exciting as we had expected so after a light lunch we board another coach to Alusia. The seventy kilometre trip only costs $1 each. I have a really big problem getting to the bus depot; Trev has gone off and left me to transport the case of rum that we bought earlier. I have to carry my backpack and the rum and I am absolutely knackered by the time I get there. All I want to do is drop into a seat but when we get on the bus all the seats are taken. Not to be outdone I put my pack on the floor and sit on it; within moments the conductor tells me to move. I think he's about to kick me off the bus, but no; instead he turns off an elderly Indian couple who are sitting on the back seat to make room for Coral and me. Coral, since the recent departure of the skipper, has become my new big-bosom-buddy.

We arrive at Alusia at 1700 hours and soon find rooms in a hostel costing $3 a night. It is basic but clean and after a light meal I am invited to share a room with Coral. I have a good night's sleep once the waves stop breaking on the beach.

Our plan is to take a journey into the Andes on a very old steam train but low cloud makes it impossible to see much; we decide to carry on to Cuenca instead. This place is about 120 kilometres away, the fare $4each. We find a typical Spanish-style hostel for $5a night. This spacious hostel is built in a square with a large open garden in the centre. Every morning we are treated to an excellent breakfast that we enjoy eating in the garden; it is inclusive of the $5 charge. In the evenings we are allowed to use the kitchen and equipment to prepare our own food. We catch onto this straight away and buy food to cook our own dinner, together with plenty of wine. When the food and wine inspires thoughts of romance Coral and I take to our bed for an early night.

We do take some entertaining walks around town visiting one or two pleasant bistros but mostly we sit beside the river chatting. All in all we share a lovely time together.

We see there is a tour from Cuenca to an Inca settlement about 64 kilometres away, book on it and off we go. The place is well preserved and we spend a long time looking around. Apparently the only people who lived there were priests, soldiers, and temple virgins, until the Spanish conquistadors arrived and changed everything. It is alleged that they killed all the men and families on or around the temple; they then raped the women before killing them too. There is a mass grave in the courtyard that is filled with the bodies of the luckless females. The lucky ones made their way to the top of a high precipice and threw themselves to their deaths before they suffered the same fate at the hands of the Spaniards; it is said several hundred females took this way out.

I meet a very old couple in a tiny cottage and along with the guide am shown some artefacts they found in the ruins. I buy a small carved stone from them suitable to be made into a pendant.

The next day we fly to Guayacil; two taxis to the airport are booked for 0430 hours, early, but it turns out to be a good thing we have time to spare as neither of the taxis turn up. We find ourselves wandering around town laden with bags and carrying slightly less rum than before; well, in the case anyhow. Luckily we find a taxi that takes us to the airport where we are joined by the *Da Capo* crew for the flight. They leave us again on landing and go straight back to the boat in Salinas but Coral and I prefer to stay and look around the city before returning. It is still very early so we go into the building that houses the travel agency we used earlier and have a couple of hours sleep lying in the stairwell outside the office. When Karen the agent arrives we leave our kit with her and take a walk around, visit a café then board a bus for the journey back to Salinas.

I meet a gorgeous young Ecuadorian lady on the bus who is suffering badly from what seems to be a severe beating to her face. We can't converse but I know lots of other ways to give her a bit of comfort as Coral sleeps throughout the journey. At Salinas the young lady gives an open display of tears as I leave her.

I take Coral along the sea front and find a café-bar where we have a good time that is repeated for several more days.

Arriving back at the boatyard we hear that there is to be a barbecue at the end of the pier. The fact that it is also Ady's birthday calls for a double celebration. The crew from the *Tree Of Life* provide the entertainment playing their didgeridoo's and we have an excellent evening. It is late when we finally make it back to the boat but I still manage a bit of crew bonding with Coral.

It is time to get stuck into something entirely different the next morning; jobs need to be done on *Antinea*. The boat is like a tip due to the electrician working on her but tidying up is out of the question yet; I have to repair the folding prop and fix a faulty shower pump. By the time the jobs are done the sun has crossed the yardarm so off we go to the beach.

We partake of the amber nectar before entering the sea; the shore temperature is 105 degrees and the water is about 80 degrees. It's amazing what comes up when bathing with a fit blonde in heat like this; we satisfy our intense, mutual desire right there and then in the Pacific Ocean. Later we return to the bar where we are rinsed down with jugs of fresh water by the staff. A couple more beers and then its back to the boat for us. There we find that the electrician has locked us out but I manage to wriggle my way in and open the hatches.

Ady comes to let us know they will be departing the next day and invites us to a leaving party in town. We all have a good evening out together before again being invited for drinks back on their boat; I decline as I am on a promise from Coral.

The night proves to be rather hot and sticky so we throw open all the hatches; but then it must have rained as we have taken quite a bit of water on board and have to clean out the bilges. I get stuck into anti-fouling the hull and also stuck into George; I give him a bollocking over the lack of progress on the boat. After completing anti-fouling half of the hull I down tools and off Coral and I go for another afternoon on the beach; we wave the *Da Capo* crew off on their way before we leave.

I find a phone and call Tracey, my son Kevin's partner, back home. Since I embarked on this trip it's been one of my great delights to hear her voice, especially now after such a long time.

We have a few beers and a swim then decide it is time to stock up for the next leg of our voyage. We do this by taking 500 cans of beer back to the boat. Next day I finish the anti-fouling and then I check the progress on the rudder. It is pleasing to see George working on it but I still tell him to get his act together and speed up on the other jobs. My next task is to clean out the contaminated fuel tank but Coral reminds me it is Sunday and maybe we could do something different, so I take her skinny dipping at the local beach. Trev sends an e-mail telling me that they are having a poor time mainly due to the weather not being too kind; it has turned a bit cool in Salinas too but I have something to keep me warm and forget all about the bad weather.

Most of my jobs on the boat are done so we get away to the beach again; we are now regularly leaving our kit behind the bar while we bathe so we're not tied up as much by having to keep an eye on it all the time. This allows us to spend more time just having fun. The bar staff once again rinse us down with cold water, then we call at a café for a Thai meal and some wine. We arrive back at the boat to find that *Tree of Life* is having a last party before leaving for the Galapagos. We are already swinging and have a great time; when we leave it is in a party mood that carries on when we return to the boat. I think we continue partying most of the night too and when we awake next day we carry on again.

George makes out that he is having trouble getting the spinnaker repaired, so I tell him that Trev will soon be returning and we want to be away. Afternoon comes and off we go to the beach again; we have the usual few beers and then, maybe due to working a night shift, I fall asleep on the sands beside the water. Coral leaves me there for over an hour and by the time I wake up the tide has gone out leaving me high and dry.

I go to check the internet and I am delighted to find that my mate Jim has got in touch; I write him an e-mail including a full tale of my escapades so far. Later, after we have got back to the boat, we hear a noise at the top of the mast. I look up and see a great big frigate bird standing on our windex. I shake the backstay until it flies off but shortly after it returns and I have to shake it off again. This goes on again and again for quite a while until it gets fed up and flies on to the next boat, but not until it has broken the arrow on our windex.

Coral and me decide to have an early night as we have been indulging in G and Ts; I must have been a bit o t t as I wake during the night to find that I am being taken firmly in hand. I wake again about 1015 hours to find the situation is still the same. "What a good start to the day." Is the thought that runs through my mind.

During our cruise I had told several short anecdotes at our many parties and one of these seems to have stuck in most minds.

"A young buck is chatting up his girl friend in the hopes of a bit of sex. She makes the excuse that she has no idea what to do, so he tells her to 'shout if it hurts and to sing if she likes it.' Shortly after she is heard to break out with "Oh, my name is McNamara, I'm the leader of the band." Well this particular morning I am doing a few jobs on *Antinea* when Rosie, the old lass off the next boat, stops for a chat. She tells me,

'Do you know, Arthur, you and your wife make a lovely couple?'

'Oh, aye",

'Yes,' Rosie replies. 'She seems a really happy woman; I've just left her singing her head off in the shower. Well, I'd better get on with my work, I'll see you later Mr McNamara!'

The weather becomes very hot so off we go to the beach again, but this time we catch a public bus, which only costs about fifteen cents and gives us a tour around local homes. It is a real eye opener into how very poor the people are as we witness the appalling conditions they live in. We have our usual few pints and a swim and then I meet a very nice Columbian woman who is instantly struck with me. We have quite an interesting chat until her husband comes on the scene to chase me off.

Taking an opportunity to call at the shopping centre on our way back to the marina we buy twenty bottles, but at the check-out I cadge a box to put them all in. As I pick up the box three bottles fall through the bottom making a proper mess of the store floor. The staff seem to be very nice about it but we are taking no chances and as they clean up the mess we disappear discreetly into the crowd.

That night we are absolutely plagued with mosquitoes but Coral takes control again and we soon find something interesting to do to take my mind off insects. Trev is due back tomorrow and will be bringing his wife Carole and their daughter; it is time to see Coral off the boat and away for the duration. The weather is miserable when we awake so after breakfast I walk to the main road and get a taxi to take her into town. She has booked herself on a cruise that will take her to the Galapagos Islands for an organised tour and then she will rejoin *Antinea* and Trev for the long voyage to French Polynesia. Trev arrives with his wife and daughter in the back of a pickup. By now the mosquitoes have become so unbearable that we all book into a hotel until the boat is ready.

Trev gets stuck into George's ribs over the way the repairs are dragging on so things then start to move a bit faster. We need to check out through immigration and this turns into a proper farce. We find the office but no officer. We hear that other staff found him so drunk in his office that there will be no checking-out today. We try again later and find him in the bar again but manage to persuade him back into his office; for twenty minutes he is absolutely adamant that there is no way we can check out as our papers are not in order. In the end Trev puts $20 on his desk and he stamps both our passports without even a cursory glance through them. This proves to be the way the whole country is run; there are seventeen political parties so the government is constantly changing. Towns are run by a local mafia and even the children who clean shoes are controlled by these villains who take all the money they make, just giving them a little food in return.

Whenever there is a cabinet meeting in parliament it is hardly ever held to discuss the state of the country but just to sort out each politician's share of the takings. The roads here all appear to be only half finished and this is because most of the roads are built with aid from other countries. The estimates put in by contractors are accepted then the prime minister asks for his share back. The contractor is left with a shortfall of cash and can only do part of the job but all involved are happy. The losers are once again the poor people and those poor sods that pay taxes to the EEC.

We sort out supplies for the voyage then the workers in the marina are on a go-slow again. I take Trev's wife Carole and daughter Sarah into Salinas for more supplies and fishing tackle and also send an e-mail off to Coral giving her the date to be back at the boat. I get a pleasant surprise; my American friend Virginia has sent me an e-mail so I reply filling her in about the present voyage.

Finally after a great deal of palaver the boat is returned to the water only for us to find that the engine isn't charging the batteries and the autopilot doesn't work. George is nowhere to be found and Trev is furious. We fuel up and fill the water tanks while waiting for the electrician to come and sort us out.

In the meantime George arrives with his bill for $7700; it is a very large amount for the work that's been done but after a lot of arguing it is greatly reduced and we are once again on our way.

The voyage is to be 570 miles and starts well enough but we are in for a surprise; we encounter fishermen about twenty miles out. It is night-time and there are miles of nets to avoid; it seems that our every move is foiled by more and more nets. We actually have to sail off course for over an hour before we round them, only to find ourselves amongst another lot a couple of hours later.

The fishermen are more helpful this time and guide us through narrow gaps between their nets, but by then we are quite a long way off course. I take over the watch at 0600 hours; in twelve hours I calculate we have covered sixty miles but only advanced forty-five along our plotted course. I am quite surprised how cold it is becoming. The water temperature is still 26c but the sky is overcast and the wind really biting.

We let out a fishing line and around 1100 hours I land a 25lb dorado. It is a beauty and goes down a treat; we have several good meals from it. By the 1st of April we are having a brilliant sail. I stand watch 2000 to 2400 hours then have a good kip till 0700 hours; the rest of my watch is uneventful; I spend most of my time enjoying the sunshine and making the boat go faster.

More trouble with the damn water-maker; the fittings that George got for us are not the right type and leak but I manage to do a temporary job on it. Later when we get in touch with Ady on the satellite phone he tells us that we will have no bother getting spares in the Galapagos.

We are down to the last 300 miles and going well. The next new day there isn't a cloud in the sky but we have to motor sail. Our ETA is in thirty-two hours.

We see a school of whales passing ahead and one surfaces about 30ft away on our port beam before swimming off slowly into the distance. We settle back to normal after the whales have gone, then we see an amazing sight; a large fishing vessel appears towing four large dugout canoes. They are going to a netting area. At the present time we are more than 250 miles from land. It must be a hard life for the guys who work from the canoes as they have no protection whatsoever from the weather and there isn't much room in the canoes to carry food or water.

We pole out the Genoa and our speed picks up to 7.5 knots. I have a big appetite at dinner which is most unusual; I really enjoy the plateful of chilli and mash that Trev dishes up. During the night I see the Southern Cross for the first time and at the same time discover that Ursa Major and other constellations that can be seen from England are now upside-down to the way I am used to seeing them. Ady tells us he is due to leave the Galapagos as he has to meet a deadline in French Polynesia in order for Sue Lane to join *Da Capo*. Trev tells me that the other Sue, Don's wife, has already left the boat in Ecuador. I am surprised to hear she's gone.

Chapter 7

Santa Cruz

I wake up on the 4th to peace and quiet. The engine is off and we are sailing at 6 knots. We are in amongst the islands now with San Christobal away to starboard and our destination Santa Cruz is only twenty-five miles away. However this turns out to be one of Trev's miscalculations. On reaching this particular way-point we find it to be nothing more than that, a way-point; we still have another eighteen miles to go. A way-point is a position marked on the chart at either the destination or at various points en route. These same co-ordinates are installed in the Global Positioning System which will then track our position by satellite and guide us from one way-point to the next.

At 1630 hours we arrive at our destination dropping two anchors over the bow. This seems prudent at the time but is to turn out to be a near disaster. Santa Cruz looks beautiful and when we get ashore we find it really is beautiful; due to the strict controls on visitors the countryside is totally unspoiled. It is unlike any other place we have seen in the whole of Ecuador; the roads are fully made up and everywhere is kept clean and tidy. After a few cold beers ashore and an easy passage through customs, we have a lovely barbecue on the boat; however we do have a lot of trouble getting it lit but eventually succeed and celebrate our arrival by having a proper piss-up.

Early next day we go off to find the fuel dock. We don't find it but we do meet a lad who takes us to a garage to fill our drums. He turns out to be some sort of travel agent and even though he organises a disastrous day out for us his wife is very helpful in getting us through immigration by telling us the only way into the country is by bribing the policeman in charge. At the same time we gain access into the national park without paying the usual fee of $100.

Our first tour is into the wilds where we see several giant tortoises and they are massive. I really find it hard to believe that one is over 350 years old; it must have been around at the time of Captain Cook. They have been reduced to near extinction by sailors and whalers who have taken them by the hundreds to provide fresh meat on their ships. I read a tale about Nantucket whalers who sent a longboat ashore to collect tortoises, but the guy in charge of the hunt set the vegetation alight as an excuse when he couldn't be bothered to catch any. The whole island got burnt with most of the animals dying in the inferno.

We take a walk down a lava tube, which is lava that has spouted out of the side of the volcano when it was erupting and then hardened forming a hollow tube. This is another first for me.

Da Capo contacts us again; they have gone for their first three days without any wind and have made little headway while we on *Antinea* are having a splendid time.

We find the islands to be fairly expensive after the prices we have been used to on the mainland but after all, the place is a tourist attraction and we are really enjoying ourselves.

We need to rise at 0400 hours to join our second tour; we are taken by bus across the island then have a two-and-a-half-hour sail to another island. Everyone is wrecked by the time we get there as the day is so hot and the early start has made us feel even worse. The island that we visit must be the newest in the group as it is still very volcanic and filled with craters and little sign of vegetation. We climb to the top of a volcano and even though the view is great the effort of doing it is just too much and as our guide speaks only Spanish we learn very little from the experience. The highlight of our day is going to a beach and swimming to cool down.

We are given a light lunch before setting out on the tedious return voyage; more despondency sets in when the boat engine starts playing up adding further to the time it will take to get back. During the journey the heavens open and we have torrential rain. Then, to top it all, the engine finally gives up the ghost just as we get close; we now have to be shipped ashore in dinghies. It is 1730 hours by the time we get back to town and we are soaked to the skin. I call at an internet cafe and contact Jim before we return to *Antinea* for an early night; I think the tour deserves a score of no more than two out of ten points.

Several boats leave overnight including *Tree Of Life* that we met earlier but we have several more days to go before leaving. We take a visit to the Darwin Centre followed by a dip in a nice little bay and later we take a very long walk to Turtle Bay. It is two miles through jungle and although there is a decent footpath it is still very tiring; a nice swim in the sea makes us all feel better but that good feeling is quickly forgotten when we start the long trek back.

As we are leaving the dinghy dock we pass the runabout boat from a cruise ship. Imagine my surprise when Coral stands up in it and waves to me.

The time eventually comes for Carole and Sarah to leave us and return home; I miss them as they have both been very nice company. They take a bus to the airport then Trev and me knock off a few outstanding jobs on the boat. In the main it is a wasted exercise as most of the time things keep going wrong so we decide to have a few beers instead. Trev gets an e-mail from Coral who tells him that she has been to Quito airport where by chance she met up with Carole and Sarah; she tells him that she's spilled the beans about him. Actually I think she is just winding him up and if she is it certainly works; he is in a daze for a couple of days.

It is time to make preparations for our next voyage; there are spares to get, gas bottles to fill, and the water-maker to fix and, finally, provisions to purchase. This job has to be thought out very carefully as buying the wrong provisions can be as disastrous as not getting enough. Our fresh greengroceries come from a small local shop where we know the produce comes straight from local farmers and lasts much longer than that sold in the supermarkets. The woman in the shop is so overcome by the size of our order worth a $140 that she gives us some sweets and chocolate. She then has second thoughts and now gives us hugs and kisses; it must be the most cash she's ever seen all in one lump.

I send off e-mails to Jim and Virginia while Trev is clearing customs then we stow all our food. Fresh fruit and vegetables hang from the cabin roof in small hammocks; this offers two benefits: the air can circulate through everything and it is easy to see any item turning bad before it spoils any others. Among other things we have bought a large quantity of vinegar and salt which in time will be a godsend in the preservation of fish and vegetables. We also take four gallons of gin in two and a half litre bottles together with several cases of wine and three hundred cans of beer. The tonic water will have to come on another trip ashore with the dinghy. Unfortunately Trev loses his bifocals over the side and spends a fruitless hour searching the sea bed in his diving gear. We are now ready to go; the time has arrived to begin our epic voyage.

When we try to raise the anchors we find them tangled; it takes us three and a half hours to separate and get them back on board. I actually have to hoist the chains up the mast on a halyard in order to untangle them, but eventually at 2330 hours on 9th April we motor into the open ocean with no wind and 3600 miles of sailing to our next stop.

My first watch is 0300 to 0830 hours during which time Trev has a call from Carole and Sarah; it isn't the one he has been expecting although he turns slightly pale when they mention having a bad time at Quito Airport. They were asked to pay $50 departure tax, but they hadn't enough cash with them. Trev had relieved them of any surplus before they boarded the bus on Santa Cruz. They were told that if they had no money then they would not be leaving; Sarah had her credit card with her and managed to raise the fee after a wild dash to the nearest bank, but the good news is that they are now safe at home in Doncaster.

At 0100 hours we get some wind and are soon under sail doing a steady 7 knots. This keeps up and at the end of our first twenty four hours we have moved on 160 miles. We have only seen one ship during that time, but we see a rare and wonderful sight this evening: a pack of dolphins in hunting mode. There are about one hundred and fifty of them and every one is absolutely frenzied; they cover a very large area and are jumping out of the water en masse to create a great disturbance. This scares the fish below and makes them cluster into a protective ball; when this occurs, the dolphins dive and devour them in dozens. It is another sight I shall never forget. We then both have a good drink before falling asleep. By the time we wake up we have covered quite a few more miles and our roast chicken dinner is burnt to a frazzle; we vow never ever to do that again.

We pass through a bad storm overnight and have to ease the main. I awake at 0830 hours to find we are doing a good 8.75 knots and are dead on course. After passing through a bad squall during the day, we saw several others in the radar and were able to avoid them.

I start with a bout of stomach pains that goes on for hours before settling down and then I manage to sleep from 2000 to 0300 hours. Ady gives us a call informing us of his position; he is exactly one thousand miles ahead and away to the south. Our weather is still good with a sea flat and we are nearing the south equatorial current which should give us an extra half knot. It's not much but over a couple of weeks or so it adds up.

I am starting to feel a little better; over the past twenty-four hours I have only eaten half an egg followed by two coffees and a can of beer.

It's quite amazing how your mind begins to play tricks when on night watch; unless there is a moon then the blackness around is total, apart from phosphorescence in the water. Trev thinks he can see a rock and is about to take avoiding action when he realises that it not only can't be true but that he is facing astern at the time. Overnight I eat a bar of chocolate that the woman in the Galapagos gave us; it goes down a treat and the next morning after a shave and shower I am once again feeling great, so good in fact that I eat a breakfast of wild passion fruit and yoghurt, the fruit being one of many that we found on our trip to see the tortoises.

We are now into preserving our fruit and vegetables otherwise we could be in danger of a food shortage; we have pickled kidney beans, carrots, cauliflower, onions, and something that looks like courgettes. We also salt our remaining cabbage and lettuce. One morning we find two dead squid on the deck that have been washed aboard overnight. We try them for lunch and find them delicious; after that we find many more appearing like manna from heaven. We have on board a fresh water-maker but it gives no end of trouble so any chance we get we store water in containers just in case it ever packs up altogether.

One big rule that we never ever break is to open a can of ale before beer o'clock. Luckily this can be anytime between 1000 and 1300 hours and woe-betide anyone on watch who forgets to waken the other at this crucial time of day. Trev bakes banana bread to subsidise our food; it's a mixture of bananas that have gone too soft to eat raw, with rum, dried fruit, flour and water. The loaves taste similar to Christmas cake and are a welcome addition to our diet as normal bread doesn't keep very long.

After my next watch I wake at 0830 hours to find that we are now sailing in excess of 10 knots; it is a poor day and the bloody water-maker has burst another pipe. I study the job out again and decide that more of it has been wrongly installed. I move the pressure control tap from its present position and fit it to the end of the membrane, and from then on we have fewer problems.

We've been so preoccupied that beer o'clock doesn't arrive until 1300 hours, an almost indefensible error. We have found a lot more squid on the deck which we eat for lunch; then for dinner we eat pickled Dorado that was caught twelve days ago proving that preserving food is paying dividends.

All through the day it has been raining on and off but we are still maintaining over 9 knots. Our morale is very high and oddly enough we have cut down on our drinking. I have only smoked two or three cigars since we set off at the beginning of January as I am also losing the taste for them. My weight has gone down and I've shed three inches off my waist; I feel superb and very fit.

On the night of April 13th the wind rises to 30 knots and we fairly scoot along. At 0500 hours the radar shows a very large storm ahead but it has moved away before we reach the position. The 14th is an ideal day with flat seas so we use this opportunity to put the engine on and make water. Everything is working perfectly now and we soon have plenty of water in the tanks. I find six dead squids today that we pickle for later use. We then we spend a lazy day sunbathing and sipping wine.

Carole phones us and tells me that Tracey has been in

contact with her and has been brought up to date on our progress. We are still knocking up 8 knots having sailed over 900 miles; at about 2000 hours we see a light off the port bow which proves to be another yacht. It is the first we have seen since leaving the Galapagos. He is going east and we watch it for a further three hours. Trev is not feeling very tired so he lets me have about five hours very welcome sleep.

We are still managing to cut down on the drinking during the day and are both feeling fine. April 15th. Still doing 8 knots; another yacht passes to port heading east at about 0530 hours. We have been going through intermittent squalls and dying winds for the past three hours then just as dawn is breaking we come across a fishing vessel laying nets across our course. We have to drop the sails and motor off course quickly until we are clear of him, the trouble being that he appears to be trying to encircle us. It is essential for us pass in front of him to be certain of avoiding his nets but he increases his speed; however we eventually get clear away and are able to get back on course. We've just got the sails back up and are making 8 knots when there is sudden loud bang; the baby stay has broken so we use a halyard as a jury rig and this is to last until we reach Raiatea on 1st June. We are also trailing an extremely heavy fishing line out astern as we can't afford to risk not landing a fish through having a weak line. A while later we hear another very loud bang and feel the boat lurch; the tracer and lure have gone but we are both glad it is the big one that got away.

Our times are now seven hours behind GMT and at 0630 hours we see a very large cruise ship that appears to be heading in the direction of San Francisco; it is something quite different to hold our attention and we watch until it disappears over the horizon. It is then time to charge the batteries and make more water. We sail all night long at 8 knots and get a beautiful start to the next day so I have a spell on the foredeck topping up my all over tan, then I give Trev a No. 2 hair cut that suits him really well.

There is a new meal on the menu today; chicken and flying fish broth. It's very tasty too and for sundowners we have a champagne celebration but can't remember what we are celebrating; however it leaves us feeling a little fuzzy for a while. It is about this time that the repeater log stops working; I can't find the fault but we have no trouble navigating.

We had originally intended making the Island of Hiva Hoa in the Marqueses our first port of call but Trev has been reading a pilot that said we would find a much better anchorage at Nuka Hiva and also a bigger variety of supplies. I read it too and discover that when Captain Cook was there he actually became in danger of losing his ship.

The girls were so promiscuous that their favours could be obtained for as little as a single nail and his ship was soon in danger of falling apart, so grudgingly I agree that it could well be the best choice. We search our tool boxes attempting to find a few nails. There is even talk of adopting some fine young native girl and taking her along with us; desperate men have desperate ways. It's unbelievable the things that go through your mind when you have hours on end with nothing to do, but now thinking in retrospect, er...what can I say?

We have another good sailing day and have just fallen short of two hundred miles in the past twenty-four hours; the next day we are to cover two hundred and four. One day we pass an odd-looking marker buoy, and then we see a ship approach it and it makes us begin to wonder if it could maybe be a drug pickup or something similar.

At long last our fresh food has completely run out; it is now time to try some of our home-produced mixed pickles, which turn out to be perfect. We have made our vegetables last at least two weeks. A cruise liner passes us about four miles off and heading NNE. It makes a bit of a change, breaking the monotony for a short while.

We are now less than 1000 miles from our first way-point and getting a little excited; the next day brings more wind, 30 knots of it giving us a speed of 9.5 knots. When we get wind strength in this range things start to heat up a little; the spray can reach right back to the cockpit as we dive into the swell and at times we are actually diving a meter or so under the water. That's all very well if you haven't to work on the foredeck and as it happens we have a very successful day.

Our meal for lunch is a mixture of pickles and squid in tomato sauce and I can thoroughly recommend it; when you're running low on fresh food it's surprising what you have to turn your hand to. We concocted all sorts of mixed food and came up with some very tasty surprises; I also discover a fine method of doing the laundry. I tie it on the end of the fishing line and let it trail out for a few hours and believe me it is spotless and smells fine afterwards, only needing a quick rinse in fresh water. The sun does the rest.

Ady rings to say that he has just blown the top off his spinnaker, but we have been reluctant to use ours as we've been doing so well without it, averaging 200 miles a day since setting out, so enough said.

Over the next night the wind increases above 30 knots but eases by morning so we change our minds and decide to put up the spinnaker after breakfast. Our choice for that meal is fresh fruit that had been steeped in rum for two weeks, excellent but HIC! We hoist the spinnaker taking over half an hour to get it up as it seems to get caught everywhere. During the afternoon we catch a four-foot seven inch-long barracuda and it puts up a tremendous fight before giving in. We haul it onto the diving platform and leave it there for nearly half an hour until it is lying perfectly still and we are confident that it's dead.

Wrong again; when Trev climbs down to take out the hook it takes a sudden lunge and bites a very large piece of flesh out of his foot. The wound is a real mess and we have a hard job stemming the flow of blood. I can only do this by packing the wound with cotton wool and then binding it tightly then leaving it until the whole dressing is totally saturated with blood. This quickly dries hard in the hot sun and stems the wound from further bleeding; a few hours later I am able to clean it all up and dress it properly. We are horror struck when we think what the outcome could have been if it had severed an artery but actually it heals very well over a time leaving not much of a scar. We share a piece of the fish about a foot long for our tea; it is very tasty but what a price to pay for it.

We have a right job later with the spinnaker; it is night time when the halyard breaks near the shackle and the dammed thing blows forward. It happens so quickly that we can't avoid sailing straight over it. One clew has to be released and we let it take its own time to float free out behind the boat before we are able to winch it onto the deck; it looks so badly damaged that we just bag it up and stow it away.

By morning we are down to just less than 500 miles to go when the weather changes for the worse. We have one squall after another and during one storm we have 50 knots of wind; we are also plagued by instant wind direction changes and have to keep gybing. We've been kept so busy that we completely forget our breakfast and have to settle for a thick broth for lunch.

The wound on Trev's foot has at last started knitting together which is a great relief. In one storm the main compass and mounting fall apart; I soon have it back in one piece but it is a tricky task while trying to keep a good hold on the boat at the same time. Conditions ease later as the wind dies down then during the late afternoon it ceases to blow altogether; we have to start the engine and motor sail all through the night. It turns out to be a bad time to be on watch, too; the Genoa drum jams but there is really no need to shorten the sail. I decide that it is too rough to attempt to clear it in the dark alone. We are hit by a string of squalls next after which we end up on a beat.

Next morning I have to go and clear the jammed reefing drum but first we have to move the dinghy off the anchor locker to gain access and all the while the bow is diving into the swell filling the locker up to my neck. The best thing I do after fixing the drum is to have a hot shower and a good sleep.

When I awake another yacht is off our port beam. We are doing 9.5 knots and leave it behind. Very soon we are up to 11.5 knots in some really high seas when out of the blue the auto helm ceases to work. It is a total disaster. We both have to take turns to steer the boat and it is very hard work. Trev has a new servo unit on board but under the present conditions it is virtually impossible to work between the cockpit sole and the hull to fit it as the boat is being thrown about violently. I have to wait until the weather eases then lo and behold it is working again; we celebrate with a couple of cold beers. From then on we sail the next twenty-four hours with the Genoa poled out but when day breaks I notice a stay has slid out of the mainsail. We have to lower the sail to fix it and neither of us has seen the type of fitting before but we fathom it out and are quickly back in action. The trade winds blow from the north east at a constant average of 27 knots while the troughs in the sea are an average of 15ft, so fore and aft the swells are higher than our boom. Our speed is 9.5 knots when I awake on the 25th remaining the same for most of day.

About 1900 hours we are hit by a very bad squall but we have the main well reefed down ready for it. Later, following a wind change, we gybe onto a direct course for the island; we are getting to be dab hands at reefing down which helps if one is hard pressed as we often are.

I watch on as a big shark swims alongside and is chased away by a school of the biggest dolphins I've ever seen. They stay with us for a while leaping completely clear of the water. Their show is an impressive performance. By now we are both looking forward to reaching land even though we've done the trip in record time. The weather has suddenly turned cold and we have to wear our jackets for the first time.

Our first sight of land is at 0500 hours April 26th. We drink coffee and remain awake; I suppose the truth is that we just want to gaze at it as any sight of land is terrific after so many miles at sea. The first island is given a very wide berth as there are large rocks scattered far and wide and the local charts are over 200 years old. When the sun comes up this morning so does the wind and reaches 35 knots. We reef both sails and still keep our speed at 9 knots.

Chapter 8

Nuka Hiva

Eventually we see Nuka Hiva and as we home in what a beautiful sight it is; all the islands are volcanic with high hills covered in dense green vegetation and they are very picturesque, enhanced by the odd basalt pillar or volcanic peak. Taiohae Bay is a perfect anchorage surrounded by high mountains and about a mile long; it is also a real sun trap, being very sheltered. We have an hour reunion on *Da Capo* exchanging our experiences then we finish the night getting stoned.

I wake up at 0400 hours in the cockpit absolutely saturated by rain before going to bed. Oddly we both have forgotten to eat the night before and are starving when we awake; a big breakfast soon puts everything right.

We meet Sue Lane once again and at first I really like her but it isn't to last. She makes it clear that she is too good to be on our boat but that is to prove to be a bad misjudgement on her part.

After clearing through immigration I am pleased to find that a $1000 bond imposed on visitors to French Polynesia is waived due to us being Brits and in the EEC. I reflect that it's the first time my country's membership has done me any good.

One thing that stands out in my mind is the fact that after a long voyage one loses partial use of the legs. This, accompanied by a certain feeling of light-headedness, can give the impression to land lubbers that the sufferer is permanently drunk. However once back on the boat these sensations disappear instantly; but for Trev it is too late, these temporary afflictions linked with his dodgy hip have already gained him the title of 'Grasshopper'.

Returning to the boat we begin essential repairs. I fix some broken alternator mountings and soon we are charging the batteries and making water. I also lay a stern anchor from the dinghy, which brings the bow up to wind leaving the boat very stable. While fitting the sail cover, I see a large tear has appeared in the luff of the mainsail; another job for the future. We join *Da*

*Ca*po for a reunion party and have a very good night. During the get-together we discuss our next move: a short visit to Hua Pou.

As we are preparing to leave a French girl comes over the VHF. She would like to join a boat going to New Zealand. We invite her over for a chat and she says she will join us when we return. We take what she says with a pinch of salt as we've heard it all before. While taking up the anchor Trev loses yet another pair of glasses.

The voyage to Hua Pou is only about thirty miles but on the way across Ady's dinghy turns turtle and he loses his fuel tank. We arrive and anchor in a very pretty bay surrounded by wooded hills but the big attraction is six massive volcano cores that have eroded into different shapes giving a lunarscape impression.

We spend an hour on the island; the people are so very friendly and gather on the jetty to help us ashore. Huge breakers have to be overcome when leaving the dinghy but the islanders are used to it and even lift the dinghies from the water. There is a small community straddling a shallow river where all the houses have natural gardens filled with beautiful flowers and fruit trees. We take quite a while exploring the place before returning to the boats. Ady joins us and brings some of his special jellies made with neat vodka. I wake up in the cockpit later but under the table and with a slightly thick head. After breakfast the anchor is raised and off we sail to the Baie D'hakahetau six miles away on the same island. On the way I tow my shorts through the sea on a line to clean them but forget to take them in before our arrival and while dropping the anchor they get wrapped around the prop. Don has to dive and clear it for us.

We go ashore for a walkabout. The place is exquisite with many very secluded bungalows, all without windows and all with gardens of wild flowers and fruit trees. I collect a few wild limes that have fallen on the village green and we use them later in our G and Ts. We return ashore in the evening for a Chinese meal at a cafe then take a dinghy dodgems ride back to *Da Capo* for late night drinks.

April 30th and today is my 64th birthday. Trev and me go to change some money. There is only one girl in the bank and everyone has to sit waiting in a queue outside. I try to use my credit card but it doesn't get accepted. It's the last thing I need but at least I have with me quite a lot of US dollars and some sterling that will pull me through. We all meet up later on the beach and play frisbee; soon lots of children gather around and quite a few of them join in the game with us. We take a long walk to see Tikas (images) being carved in wood but they are so expensive that no one buys any.

I fix up the barbecue on the boat and everyone joins in my birthday celebrations and all of us get drunk. I still feel smashed when I awake at 0800 hours the next morning. I manage to get through on a phone to Tracey and Jess. It's lovely to talk to them again. They are to finally move to their new home on Friday May 3rd. I wasn't able to face breakfast when I got up so I go join the locals celebrating May Day with a big party in their community centre and have some food there. They are displaying local crafts and most of the women are dressed in sarongs and wear flowers in their hair. They all look absolutely gorgeous.

Our return trip to Nuka Hiva goes well sailing at a nice 8.5 knots but while approaching the bay we are hit by a squall. I find the bloody foresail drum jammed again and get drenched once more in the anchor locker. I am surprised and delighted to find Marina Jaquet, the French girl, waiting to join us. She is a lovely girl. We have a quiet evening meal then later we are joined by the *Da Capo* lot and we all have a friendly chat getting to know each other. As all the shops are closed for May Day we cannot but agree that we will have to go to do our shopping tomorrow.

I rise at 0700 hours and both Trev and Marina are up already so I shower then we all go off on the shopping expedition. I can't find any fresh vegetables so I pass the task on to Marina. Trev says,

'What if she doesn't have any idea what to get?'

When we catch up with her she's made a brilliant job of provisioning; I help her to carry the supplies back to the dock and as she slides off the dock into the RIB with her legs spread out to hit the dinghy a gust blows up her dress revealing the best credentials I've seen for a long time. We are under way within the hour but as we sail down the bay Ady calls us back on the

VHF; he has no electrics. Dropping the sails we return to help; it turns out to be a broken terminal post on one of his batteries. Luckily we have a spare and once he has it on board he's soon under way again. Our next call, Baie de Taioa Hakatea is only about an hour away; it is one of the best anchorages I have ever seen. After rounding a dog leg one is cut off completely from the outside world. We drop anchors and are soon having fun and games on the beach; that is, until the mosquitoes find us, then it's back to the boat for drinks and a chat. Later it rains heavily but we don't let it spoil our party.

May 3rd is a lovely day; the anchorage is spectacular with the early morning sun shining over it. We take the dinghies and motor to Daniels Bay; it is named after the local headman who is there waiting to guide us through the shallows into a pool were we can tie up. Daniel lives in a little old shack with his wife Antoinette; she is paralysed in the legs but still has a nice smile for everyone. They speak French as is the case with all the people on these islands but by casting my mind back a year or two to my schooldays and with a little help from Marina I am able to hold a conversation and I learn about the way they live. Of course I show my gratitude to the little frog – affectionate name for her, by teaching her some words of proper English and eventually she becomes quite fluent in the West Yorkshire language. But I do have to caution her from time to time as she often slips in a few of my more explicit bits of Yorkshire dialect when she becomes excited. You should see the colour that several faces turn when Marina comes out with them.

Daniel is well known amongst the yachting fraternity as he allows them use of his very own source of spring water to replenish their stocks. Traditionally every visiting sailor brings Daniel a T-shirt. He shows us the way to a footpath leading through the many small homesteads and deep into the mountains. Most of the homes here are beautiful with carefully maintained gardens; many of them fenced off, and although most of the fruit trees are still growing wild there are a few small plantations similar to English orchards. Several of the villagers come to say hello and give us fruit to eat on our trek. There is a shallow river beside our route which we have to cross several times on the way and due to Trev's foot still having an open wound Ady has to ford with him laid over his shoulder.

We continue along until we reach the true jungle and have to carve our way through the dense vegetation as we are trying to follow an ancient dry stone road that leads through dozens of old ruined houses. It is now overgrown with thick bushes. The population in these islands ran into many thousands before Captain Cook arrived bringing with him diseases to which they had no immunity. Soon the tribes were absolutely decimated, and now there are less than 30,000 in total living on all of the islands in the group.

We trek on for three hours until we reach a very high blind canyon in the mountains. A waterfall here is the third highest in the whole world but unfortunately when we arrive it is down to a mere trickle. However we find a deep pool at the base of the spout. Marina has most of her clothes off in a matter of seconds and dives in so we all follow; it is fabulous, very cold but very exhilarating too. After climbing over a large rock we are able to enter a cavern which contains another deep pool and swimming in that is a fantastic experience. On our way back to the village we feed well on wild mangos and coconuts.

We are all knackered on arrival but as the tide is out we have to manhandle the dinghies over a shoal into the sea. On reaching the boat we are so tired that we settle for a drink and a quiet night.

The author ‘sunning myself on the island of Atata, Tonga

‘It’s in the Guinness Book of Wots’it’ Uchutupu Pippi Island.

One up – One down, detached and semi holiday homes
in the Ecuadorian jungle.

Shell shocked in Santa Cruz, Galapagos Islands.

'I've got a Bite'
He certainly put his foot in it.

The peaks of Hua Pou - French Polynesia.

'Put me down I don't want to go'.

Tahiti from the bay.

The reef, part of Iles Huahine in the Society Islands.

A rock pool in its glory at Niue.

The author overlooking Maselema village Vavau, Tonga.

Pony trekking in the Andes.

My two Tongan friends, Ofa and Eseta, in Singapore.

Chapter 9

The Marqueses

Sat. May 4th and we are all up and away at 0430 hours and on our way to Ua Uka. The wind is 25 knots on the nose and we have no option but to motor sail. We are beating all the way with high seas crashing over us all the time and to make matters worse we never achieve more than 2.5 knots over the ground for the duration of the passage. We finally arrive at Invisible Bay, so named because if you didn't know it was there you would never see it. The entrance is narrow and choppy but, like most things that are hard to get into, very nice when you do.

We give the village an eyeball and on the way round buy a few supplies at the store for surprisingly low prices. The locals are holding a function in the community centre so we give it a visit. A meal of stewed goat and rice is served up on our arrival; yuk! There is also a can of coke presumably thrown in to kill the taste, then to end the event we are given about 50lb of bananas.

On our return to the boats everyone joins in and has a pleasant drink while I watch on and make another damned pipe for the water-maker. We are finding that Marina is the best crew member we've had; she's a little belter who puts her heart and soul into the sailing. We make arrangements to go pony trekking in the morning but overnight the dinghy breaks loose, or, as I still think, it was untied and taken to the jetty. We easily recover it so Trev gives a cap and T-shirt to a bloke who says he's rescued it, although I'm still convinced that it was more of a ransom. Our ponies are collected and we ride off for miles and miles to another bay; the journey is quite pleasant but the saddles on the horses are nothing less than torture devices. They are made of wood covered only by a piece of hessian. We arrive at our destination all suffering from a serious beer deficiency but there are a couple of restaurants so our thirst should soon be sated; or so we think. When we try to buy a few beers we are told it is Sunday and no beer is available. The horses are more successful and drink from a nearby stream while we have to stick it out until we get back.

I am absolutely knackered by then and my backside feels as if it is on fire. On the way we see lots of old stone Tikas carved by the ancients as guardian angels to keep away bad spirits; so at least we should sleep well. We are told by the man who owns the ponies that he has thirty altogether; it gets me wondering how the hell he managed to find me the most uncomfortable trotter I've ever ridden on and the laziest too; I have to whip it most of the time just to get it to move.

I soon forget my aches when I am greeted by a lovely smile from our new crewmember who I find sitting on the end of my bunk tickling my toes when I awake the next morning. She tells me about a folk museum that is to be our first port of call; it is small but good and seeing that all the locals speak French our little frog comes in very handy. Sue joins us later and Marina prepares lunch for us before we motor a few miles up the coast to another bay. It is a little exposed to say the least but about a mile away is another island, a breeding place for terns and the owners have fixed a rope on the cliff to give access to the nests. I've been awarded the dubious pleasure of climbing up it to collect some eggs but on arrival we find it is low water and I can't even reach the rope, which is maybe a good thing for me.

The beach and a swim then seem a much better option so off we go; the water is very warm and has big breakers but the undertow us the strongest I've ever come across.

Marina swims back to the boat when we've finished. She's like a fish in the water. I could sit watching her swim for hours; she just keeps on and on. We all have a cold shower on the diving platform that leaves us feeling refreshed then it is early to bed as we will be leaving at 0430 hours in the morning. As usual we are under way on time and sailing at 9 knots on a heading to Tuhuata.

The weather is ideal and we are able to enjoy breakfast out in the cockpit; since Marina joined us we have had no bother with the sails or anchor. She and I seem to work well together and she knows every time what is needed of her without having to have everything explained. Even on sail changes the sheets or the halyard will be always released at exactly the right moment as she watches my every move on the foredeck. Today we are working really well and leaving *Da Capo* way behind even though they have a crew of six. We are heeling well over to starboard and I find that water is being forced up the sink drain pipe in the heads, flooding the place. I turn off the sea cocks and then have to bucket the place dry but from then onwards it becomes common practice to turn off all the sea cocks whenever we are hard pressed. Next we get a fuel problem but as there is no operator's manual on the boat it takes us a while to sort out. We have three fuel tanks, but the two that give us trouble can be controlled by remote shut off valves, the big problem is that we don't know which lever works which valve. So previously we were advised to leave them as they were. Today we find however that when the boat heels over for a long period, fuel drains from one tank to the other and we get an air lock. Fortunately there is a spare tank on board but as usual there is another problem: the gang who modified it in Curacao did not give a great deal of thought to the pipe-work layout so it has to be primed from under the floor and invariably the floor panels are covered with spare sails etc. Eventually I have the tank connected and fuel pumped through, then once more we are up and running.

Next we want to reef the head sail but this constantly gives trouble as the reefing line will build up on the drum till the line rides over the top edge and jams the whole operation. Once again it is the same gang that fitted the new furling gear; later we fit a thinner line and this seems to overcome the problem. However at the moment the tangle has to be cleared and to do this I need to sit in the cramped anchor locker with water up to my neck as the bow dips into the waves. To top it all, the engine chooses to stop charging. By the time we drop our anchor I am totally shagged out and lie down for a rest while Marina goes out to sit in the cockpit.

Suddenly I am awakened by the sound of her screaming and hurry out on deck to join her. I am dreading what to expect but find the crew of *Da Capo* pelting her with eggs and bad bananas from their dinghy; she has been sunbathing but most of her anatomy is now a curious shade of yellow. She is an amiable lass and quickly sees the funny side of it but she still leaves them in no doubt that they are out of order; although when she shouts for them to stop it and go away it appears that she has picked up some English expressions from me. Her actual words are,

'Why don't you go and fuck off!'

To which they respond in apology that it was only meant as a joke. I hose her down and clean the boat then we declare open war on them. Later I go to the beach for a swim but I am so knackered that I lie down in the dinghy and fall asleep. I only wake up again when I am shaken so that they can all return to the boats.

The next day is a busy one too; I reconnect the fuel tanks and then I get the engine re-charging; next it is the turn of the GPS antenna to pack up on us. I have to strip and rewire it but surprisingly enough it works again; then the radar and GPS repeater go on the blink; once again it turns out to be another of Fatman's bodge jobs behind the wiring panel. Once the work is done I am left with time to sit back and take some lovely shots of Marina in her bikini.

I fit the barbecue unit to a cockpit rail as a party is on the agenda for this evening and *Antinea* is to be the venue; we all go ashore to forage for food in what appears to be an old plantation returning with quite a collection of coconuts and limes. The party is a great success; I awake next morning to find Marina's legs hanging over my porthole. When I poke a feather through and tickle them she leaps into action and attacks me in a fit of laughter.

We motor four miles up the coast to another bay although it is a real problem getting ashore as large waves keep rolling along the dock side. The only way that we can get there is to leap from the dinghy as it is swept past the jetty The effort is well worth it as the locals give us a very warm welcome; we are shown no end of carvings all expertly done but once again they are asking more money for them than the big retailers are charging so we don't buy anything. Instead we ask if they will sell us some fruit.

'No!' is the reply. 'We will only give you some.'

When the fruit arrives there are two sacks full of very large grapefruits that are really juicy and sweet; I am just eating my third when two women shin up a tree and pick us a sack of a fruit that looks like apples. These too are tasty. I give the headwoman a necklace and later Sue returns with Marina to share lots of lollipops with the children.

We are advised to move to another anchorage as the place we are in will not hold in foul weather. I beg to differ though when we try to raise the hook. It is so fast we have to motor back and forth to break it out. Our batteries are so low in charge that the bloody windlass won't lift it so we have to move with the anchor hanging far below. Once we are secure again I replace the alternator and get everything working again, leaving me time to have a bit of fun with our lovely little frog.

I think I am first awake next morning, Trev is fast asleep in his bunk but I can't find Marina. I search around and even scan around with the binoculars but still see no sign of her. Much later I hear her singing and take a look around the boat in the dinghy; there she is in the water scrubbing the hull. I give her a little bollocking and tell her to let someone know when she is going to work alone in the water again but she just sticks her thumb up and says.

'Okay, mate, point taken.'

Together now we both spend an hour scrubbing the deck and cockpit. After breakfast a lot of dolphins come around. She is in the water like a shot to join them swimming all over the place; I tell her that she is lovely but crazy. All too soon it is time to move on. We leave Tahuata about 1100 hours and motor sail at 8 knots until we reach the end of the island then change to our new course. We have a twenty-two knot wind right on the nose which cuts our speed to 3 knots over the ground; but we finish the last leg into the anchorage at Hiva Hoa with a flourish.

The Baie Atuona is a very peaceful place with lovely views all around. Our first job is to go ashore and get sixty litres of free water from a tap on the jetty. Marina always gives me a hand when there is anything to do or fetch and the same applies for this job. We do a bit of shopping too; she has been to Hiva Hoa before and as she already knows the layout we make a note to visit the internet café later as I need to make contact with the outside world again.

Marina becomes quite upset; she can't find her purse which contains her passport and money so when we get back to the boat of course she mentions it to Trev.

'When did you last see it?' he asks.

She tells him, 'It was here on the boat.'

'Well, then, there is nothing to worry about,' he replies. 'Neither of us would take it so it must still be around.'

She searches her cabin and sure enough it is there; it had dropped down the side of her bunk and under a locker. She puts on a lovely smile and gives a sigh of relief.

No place can be absolutely perfect as I soon find here; I haven't been bitten since leaving Ecuador but now I am getting eaten alive. The insects are enough to drive you bloody barmy.

While *Da Capo* was on passage here they came across two lads in a canoe well off shore so they went alongside to check them out. The lads were absolutely stoned out of their minds on pot so Ady had to unload the dinghy and tow them to the shore. We all have a great get together that night, eating, drinking and getting to know Marina.

The town is about three miles away so the next morning Marina flags down a pickup truck and asks for a lift; from then on that is to be our regular method of travelling. On arrival the bank is closed as there is a sort of fiesta on the go. The time is only 0730 hours but even at that time of day it is usual for everything to be in full swing. We buy a few more groceries and pay a visit to the internet café where I read two messages from Virginia and then stay around for a pizza and a few beers. By now it is time to visit the gendarmerie to check out. The officer there is very arrogant and because we only speak English, he begins to play on it, but he hasn't bargained for our little frog or Don.

They give him a right dressing down until his superior overhears and after giving him the hard word sorts us out in a few minutes. When we are all finished the cafe owner takes us and our shopping back to the boat in his pickup truck. That evening Marina and I carry 140 litres of water from the tap on shore filling up our tanks to the brim; we follow this by a water fight in the shower. The water is ice cold and the showerhead is a proper gusher but we really have a good time. We have now become quite close. Marina has put my e-mails on a disk so I can read them at my leisure. There is one from Ian on Chwan. He's a lad I met in the Azores and now is a good friend who writes regularly.

For dinner Trev cooks peppered steaks which we take to *Da Capo* to complement the salad Lucy has prepared. We party until late and a great time is had by all.

I am awake at 0600 hours thinking how great it is to be alive and here. I am sure it will be hard to settle down in England again after the trip and having had a completely different lifestyle like this. Returning to town we stock up with $600 worth of supplies and then call at the internet café again. On the previous day Trev asked the owner if he would save some franks and exchange $200 for him as the bank is a bit of a hit and miss option, but when we get there Sue, who overheard the deal, has been in earlier and taken all the change. Trev is understandably angry so finally she concurs to let him have half; had it been up to me I'd have wrung her bloody neck.

After lunch we go to meet Felix; he is a proper character who owns a large orchard. We take him a cheap bottle of rum we bought in Ecuador and a T-shirt. It took us quite a while to find his shack which is hidden well away from the road. He is delighted when he sees the rum and takes us on a tour of his property. He climbs several trees to collect fruit and eventually fills our two sacks with quite a variety. He also gives us some kava roots which taste foul when crushed and soaked in water but they make a strong narcotic drink. Marina puts on a show that night with her French cuisine; we eat crepes filled with eggs and tomatoes followed by more filled with her homemade jam for dessert, then later we both go in the dinghy to the dock for a shower. While we are playing around she falls on some steps and hurts her knee. She seems so concerned that I asked her what is wrong. She explains that she has poor circulation in her legs and has been advised to avoid knocks and bruises and that she will almost certainly have problems with them in later life. This is the same condition that led to my wife losing both her legs and then her life. I silently hope to God that the lass will never go through anything like that.

Everyone is up early next morning preparing to leave; we are already tanked up with water but need more diesel fuel, so we take several containers to the dock. It is a very bouncy operation as the dinghy is thrown about like a cork but eventually we get the job finished. While we are at the fuel pump Felix joins us; we have been hearing all sorts of things about him from the locals. He is of African origin and has lived here on this island for the past twenty years; he is also a retired revolutionary, one of the Contra Guerrilla's from Panama. We should have been expecting anything from him, but it comes as a surprise when he asks us if we have any spare ammunition even though it is an offence punishable with imprisonment on these islands for residents to have anything of that nature in their possession; it leaves me wondering what he is up to now.

While we've been here on the island the French elections are being held with Le Penn, a racist candidate, standing for election. It is very noticeable that he will be getting very little support here.

Once again we are all prepared for off; taking a last glance as we head south west to our next destination, the Tuamotus, 400 miles away. At first the weather is a bit mixed with many wind changes that keep us busy making sail adjustments; about 1500 hours the wind drops off forcing us to switch on the motor. Marina once again tempts our palates with another excellent lunch.

Yet again we have trouble with the roller reefing line jamming the drum. I have just got it fixed having climbed out of the anchor locker when the boat lurches causing the locker lid to drop down on my big toe, bursting it. The pain is excruciating so I use the glowing sharp end of a paper clip to pierce the nail; the release of pressure is a big relief. I lose the nail within days and even with my little French nurse's TLC it is many months before it heals up properly.

The weather is becoming hotter by the day condemning us to drink lots of water to prevent dehydration; drinking beer is not the answer, it's just nicer. Another thing to remember when sailing in the hot sun is that the breeze gives a false impression of how hot the sun is; you can easily end up badly burnt, therefore it is very important to take extra care.

Trev makes dinner. He's an excellent cook who prepares a varied range of very tasty meals; tonight's meal is no exception. We begin keeping three hour watches. That's the time when yearnings pass through your mind and during my watch I am soon feeling a bit homesick but I expect to be back in England for a break in about seven weeks. There is little wind throughout the night so we have to use the motor with just a little help from the sails.

The next day is hot again with not much wind creating another day of idleness; at first I do a lot of reading, until Marina asks if I will help her to master the tide tables. Doing this both helps to pass the time and serves as a revision exercise for me.

Trev has baked some lovely steak and onion pasties which we have with mushy peas and mash for dinner followed by Pina Colada sundowners.

Overnight the wind picks up and I am able to trim the sails, increasing our speed. We find the next time Ady calls that I have passed *Da Capo* and we are seven miles ahead. Taking a look at my shower pump, which has always been a problem, I find that a wrong size of flap valve has been fitted. I cut it back to size and it works perfectly. There have been a lot of alterations to the system so I think there must have been bother with it from it being new.

The wind picks up again bringing our speed to 8.5 knots. It is brilliant but eventually we need to put a reef in. Marina goes to the mast where I see she is having trouble with a snap shackle. Being a gentleman I go to help; the problem is that the pull string is missing so with wet fingers she can't grip the release pin. I look around for some cloth to help me to grip it but the only thing I can see that will be of use is Marina's T- shirt. The situation we are in calls for some quick action so I take hold of the bottom edge and try to reach the pin.

She shouts out, 'No! No.' then sees I need the cloth to help me to pull the pin and shouts again, 'Okay. Do it.'

Well, the shackle is high and the shirt is low and Marina

isn't wearing a bra so while I am releasing the shackle, me and Trev, who is on the helm, get a wonderful view of the little frog's tits.

Once we're back on course we go well all the day but during my night watch the wind keeps changing from a reach to a beat then back again and to top it all there is heavy rain; I am glad when it's time to get my head down.

Marina is on watch when I awake at 0630 hours and I join her for a chat then we tack the head sail and at once the boat is on the move again. There are only another forty-three more miles to our way-point when the wind picks up but we are behind time and won't make Manihi in daylight so we change course and make for Takaroa instead.

We are now among the Tuamotus, known as the dangerous islands, which are all coral atolls with most having a very narrow passé through the surrounding reef. Takaroa is no exception and the pilot has it down as being a difficult passé too, so being our first attempt at this sort of thing we are all a bit on edge. We arrive at the reef. It has three wrecked cargo ships on it and I think,

"Who's going to be next?"

There is a constant five-knot current flowing out; it could ease slightly but never flow inwards. It is no time to be hesitant so we go for it finding the passé and motoring through to the jetty with no problems. Circular reefs are usually awash so once water gets in then the only way out is through the passé resulting in the one way flow.

We are met immediately by a group of men who invite us to go on a fishing trip but we decline their offer as there is no mention of taking Marina along. We then get heavy rain and one lad tells us that it only rains two weeks in the year but this week has turned out to be one of them. Each building has a massive water butt piped to every available catchments area; usually a roof. We take a walk around the village which is really small and we are amazed to see several new pickup trucks as there are only about two miles of road on the whole island.

There is one small store and a restaurant where we intend eating out until we see that all the meals are incredibly expensive. The population can't be much more than one hundred with three women to every man but they seem to have the problem sorted as I notice the only church here is Mormon.

Quite a lot of children come around to take a look at us and are all rewarded with lollipops; however I see two very shy little girls and give them a fancy necklace each. They both stand shaking their heads slowly until Marina explains that they are gifts then they dance away happily.

We rise at 0430 hours and prepare for off; Marina speaks to two blokes on a large fishing boat asking if they will handle our mooring lines. The bow is let loose and we come about helped by the outgoing flow, then at the crucial moment the aft line is released and we are heading very quickly out through the passé. There is definitely no second chance during this manoeuvre. After motoring for an hour we let out the sails and off we go.

I know now that I am going to be very sorry if ever Marina leaves the boat. She is not just a very nice young woman but also good to have as crew and a lovely friend too. I stand first watch while the others get some sleep and we are soon doing 8 knots gull-winged. When daylight breaks I am shocked to find our ensign has been stolen and later find they've even taken Marina's sandals.

We make good time to Manihi, where again the passé has a five-knot flow. It is very narrow too but we make it even though we have to wind our way round several coral heads on the way.

Trev is getting very frustrated with Marina. He'd expected her to just drop everything for him but I like her just for who she is. She tells me that she has already figured out his problem and says that she understands how even I must be feeling too with her on board but please to wait and maybe soon?

We have a swim together in the sea. It is great but then she begins scrubbing the under bottom of the boat again.

Don will soon be leaving *Da Capo* to go to New Zealand to visit his children while I myself am very happy just seeing all my childhood dreams coming true. Imagine me in a South Pacific paradise with ninety degrees of sunshine and warm seas to swim in. I only wish I had my wife Iris here with me to share it all.

We rig the barbecue up as Don and Sue are to join us. We have a fine time as Marina has made a bowl of punch that livens up the conversation somewhat. I hear that Ady is soon to kick Sue off the boat; the bugger has been trying to palm her off on me since she arrived but I'm not having any of it; she didn't want to know us not so long ago. I am sitting in the cockpit the next day with Marina when out of the blue she asks if we can do a bit of straight talking. She then tells me.

'I don't want to leave the boat; you and me work like a good team. I would like to stay till New Zealand and who knows, maybe more?'

She goes on to tell me that when she joined the boat she'd been frightened on finding none of the girls were on *Antinea* but once she got to know me she felt very happy and at ease;. After her straight talking she hauls me up the mast to fix the lazy jacks.

The three of us go to visit a pearl farm to watch them working; it is not to be one of the organised exhibition tours but more of an impromptu one made through one of the workmen. Later we go into the village by dinghy. It is about a mile away and one has literally to climb over coral heads to get into the dinghy harbour. There is a mobile cafe beside the harbour where we can buy a beef burger and bun but it costs about £10. Every thing is extremely expensive. In the evening we go aboard *Da Capo* for drinks and I also try a puff of pot but don't reckon much to it.

Marina tells me tonight she has noticed how randy Trev and me are becoming but I am not to worry as she would like to sort something out but please to give her a bit more time. Shortly after that she becomes close to me, often coming to sneak a cuddle with me when I am on watch.

I am up and about at 0630 hours next morning and feeling as though I've been given a new lease of life, but then I start suffering from tennis elbow. My little frog asks,

'Are you sure it's not penis elbow?' I tell her maybe it is but she can help me ease the trauma.

It is then Marina's turn to feel ill; she really is under the weather so I give her a Lemsip to drink and leave her sleeping for hours. I have a short nap too as Trev has gone diving with Don and Ady. I awake when they get back but Marina is out for a further two hours and seems to be much better for the rest when she does surface; in fact she makes us a smashing paella for dinner. My elbow is getting worse with the pain carrying right up into my shoulder. Trev tells me that while he was diving he ran out of air and one of the guides had to share his with him till he got to the surface.

I get up early in the morning to do my washing but Trev and Marina stop me and they clean my clothes as my arm is now badly swollen. Overnight Ady has left a line out and caught a 3ft shark; I take a lovely photo of Marina holding it then she asks me,

'Arthur, you will come with me to see the surgery.'

Off we go to the village doctor who sends me to the home of a French nurse for treatment. She gives me pills and ointment together with advice on what to do; and all for nothing. Marina tells me the nurse has been pleased to help because while attending to me she has been able also to have a chat with her in their own language; apparently she is very homesick.

We buy two cases of beer and leave them in the shop while we stroll around the village; sadly we meet Sue and when we collect our beer she whinges until she gets to buy a case of beer also. She and Marina go to a cargo boat that is landing supplies in order to get some groceries. The goods have all to be pre-paid for and are very expensive; once paid you have to join a long queue to wait, and wait, and wait... The whole deal is a very dodgy affair as the scales are kept in an unlighted cabin and only the bloke using them can see anything. Meanwhile the locals keep passing their chits down the line by-passing Sue and Marina so by the time they get served it is pitch black.

We return to the boat very slowly in order to avoid the many coral heads and I have to tell Sue to shut her gob as we need to concentrate on watching for rocks. When we finally get back Marina is so knackered she has to go to bed. I can tell that she is still not a hundred per cent well, but, wow, what a great lass she is.

Both boats leave early the next morning for Ahe thirty-five

miles away. We find the passé easy going and motor through; once inside there is a channel to the harbour clearly marked by normal red and green buoys but for some reason or other Trev takes the scenic route and leads us into the oyster beds. Within fifteen minutes we are caught in a mass of lines on which the oysters are suspended. However we stop the engine letting the boat drift free and shortly after we are back in clear water to motor down the buoyed channel. We make it easily after that, anchoring close to the village. Ady joins us dead on cue when we break out the gin and tonics and once again the bugger tries to unload Sue onto me; I am secretly happy to have chosen my own friend.

We also get a visit from Don with an invite to a party and later join them on *Da Capo*; it is a great night but unfortunately I upset Sue. She keeps ranting on at me and talking a lot of rubbish so I tell her to shut her bloody gob and let someone else get a word in; she begins crying but leaves me alone and starts on Trev. Marina and I take the initiative and go back to *Antinea* in the dinghy for a nice chat and a lot of hugging. Apparently I am supposed to fetch Trev later on but we forget him and fall asleep leaving him to swim back at about five o'clock in the morning.

He is still asleep when we awake so it gives me the chance to have another go in the cockpit with my lovely little frog. We all go out to snorkel on a reef but I stay in the dinghy. It is quite enjoyable; with a little water in the bottom I can lie and keep cool as I sunbathe. Marina is last back to the dinghy and when she takes her mask off her saucer-sized eyes she announces,

'I met a shark. It was about four feet long; it swam up to me and just lay there staring into my face.'

She had eased away from it very slowly so as not to attract more attention but I know that she is very shocked by the state she is in. Don has also seen a shark and he is to think twice before going in again. Tonight it is our turn to do the entertaining. Marina grills steaks for dinner then we all go into the get-pissed mode. There is a lot of unease on *Da Capo* now since Tony has gone back home. Lucy has phoned her mum and been told that she doesn't want to speak to her. Tony has lost his job through being away too long, so that is another upset for them. Ady still wants Sue off his boat but as we won't take her on he looks like being stuck with her until we reach Papetee. I am only glad that *Antinea* is still a happy boat.

I awake to find Marina is up and about. She waves to me to join her out on the deck and although she is suffering from a slight hangover she carries it well, giving me a very tender kiss. Trev wakes up with a very bad head. We arranged a visit to another pearl farm last night; it involves wading across a reef under two feet of water. There is a fairly strong current and the reef is very slippery and I think we are lucky that no one falls down. Watching them at work preparing the oysters is very interesting. Tiny young oysters are caught on things that look like bottle brushes. They are hung in the lagoon and when grown they are taken to have a hole drilled through their shells to enable them to be hung out on long lines until they are large enough to produce pearls. When they reach this stage they are taken into the workshop, forced open and wedged; this gives access to make an incision into the body and insert a tiny plastic ball. The shell is allowed to close and they are returned to the sea on lines for a year after which they are taken in again and the pearl is removed and replaced by another slightly larger ball. They are able to produce pearls for three years and every year the pearls are bigger. A pearl is created when a small particle of sand or other hard material enters the oyster's body. The immune system comes into action building a layer of nacre or mother of pearl around the offending particle which constantly grows in size. On the farm they can process 10,000 per day but they have to work fast as oysters can only live for an hour out of the water.

After the demonstration we wade back to the village; I just make it back to the boat and the heads. I have been feeling a little bit off colour for a couple of days with not much of an appetite; I think my stomach nerves are playing me up again.

The shark scare certainly hasn't put Marina off her swimming and she is soon out on the reef again swimming like a fish and having a good time. We decide to go next to Rangiroa; we'll be leaving next day about 1500 hours and will have an eighty mile trip ahead of us. We've had a lovely time on Ahe. There are only about 200 people here; all they can grow is coconuts as there is hardly any depth of soil. Everything has to be imported which makes most things very expensive to purchase; everyone is fully employed either on the pearl farms, some of which were built on stilts in the lagoon, or they go out in the many fishing boats.

We have a quiet night and only eat chicken and fruit. I myself have a brief chat then I go off to bed. That is when I start my marathon night in the heads; I am up at 0600 hours and feeling a little better but have no appetite. Trev and Marina pull me up the mast in order to move the VHF aerial. Our transmissions have not been very strong of late and we hope this may do the trick. I see a badly fitted shield on top of the forestay that is fouling the Genoa halyard and fix that too while I am at it.

There has been some discussion of going to the Isle Raiatea and leaving the boat in a marina, letting our little frog Marina take care of it while we are away in England; Lucy will also be staying with her, then we'll fly to Tahiti and home.

At about 1400 hours we start to weigh the anchors. We've been expecting trouble as there are so many coral heads about and Ady's stern anchor is good and fast. Don has to dive and unwrap it for him then we pull it up while sitting in Trev's dinghy. Marina dives and swims above our anchor while I am winching it aboard. At the same time I get Trev to follow the route she is taking along the chain and in doing so we lift it up easily. It comes up like a dream even though it is threaded in and among the coral heads. We get to the passé on ebb tide going through without effort. I stand watch 2030 to 0000 hours then stay up with Marina for an hour for our usual chat. But as I am about to go to bed I am smitten again and have to rush to the heads. This goes on for the rest of the night.

Our next call, Rangiroa, is the largest atoll in the Tuamotus group and is 100 miles in circumference. One of the attractions is a hotel that puts on glass-bottomed boat trips from where people throw food to the sharks and naturally these creatures swim around the anchored boa continuously. Unfortunately for us, Trev chooses to anchor close to it throughout our stay.

Chapter 10

Rangiroa

On the voyage we try to slow the boat in order to catch the flow in the passé at its slowest but we still arrive early. The passé is described in the pilot as being very dangerous and as we inch forward on full revs we are meeting a flow of 7 knots and many over falls. Eventually we're through and it is a great relief to be in the lagoon. Everyone goes ashore at once but Marina and I stay back to rest a little. The peace is ruined when Sue calls on the VHF wanting us to join them; for the time being that is the end of that. We do however return later with a little more success.

We join them all at the internet café around midday but even this is much against my will. I have had two e-mails from my mate Jim and am pleased to hear that my boat moored in Scarborough is still all right. In return I send him a long letter about some of my escapades between here and Ecuador; also informing him of my intended visit to England.

Marina stays ashore on the internet while I go back for a drink on *Da Capo*. She calls me later on the VHF seeking to know where we are, so Lucy goes in the dinghy to fetch her things while Marina swims back to the boat.

"She's bloody barmy."

She makes half the dinner while Ady cooks beef curry then it is party time. Trev gets so pissed that he falls over stubbing his toe before landing on his head; it looks as though it could be broken.

While here we are invited to a barbecue on shore organised by visiting Yanks. We naturally put in an appearance during which I chat with their womenfolk and without realising it I become the topic of conversation throughout most of their fraternity.

Another new day and I am feeling great. Trev and Marina have gone diving while I charge and test the batteries, then I go over to the internet café and send an e-mail off to my buddy Ian on *Chwan*. Trev joins me in the internet café then I take everyone diving in the passé. I stay in the dinghy ready to rescue anyone who gets dragged into the current. Our little frog is worn out when we reach *Antinea* and goes to bed but later she's up again and makes us a lunch fit for a king. I like these occasions as we always have a good laugh.

At night we all go to the hotel where they are holding a barbecue. There have been no vacancies but Don gives the manager a bribe and gets us squeezed in. It is an excellent outing but very expensive. Marina is invited to join in with some native dancers giving a show - grass skirt and all. When we get back to *Antinea* the first thing I do is gallop to the heads; I am back to square one but we do have a good booze up to finish off the day.

Marina and Sue go to see Don off at the airport today leaving me and Trev to follow on later. We manage to hitch a lift, which is a godsend as the village is eight miles away. We meet up with Marina for a drink then buy some groceries and two slab packs of beer. Trev whispers to me, 'I don't know what Marina is playing at but she's just bought the biggest fuck-off bag of pasta that I've ever seen.'

We never give it another thought but she must have overheard him and that evening she leads us out into the cockpit while she prepares dinner. She sets the table serving cheese, pickles, and cold meat, then she brings out a big covered bowl and without any trace of a smile or expression announces.

'Voilà, Trev, now try my big fuck-off pasta special.' I still laugh whenever I think of it.

We must have had rain through the night as the air is so fresh when I wake up. Marina is already out swimming. I hear during the day that a diving party has gone out in the passé earlier and been hard pressed by a school of sharks; they were even rammed but the guide got them all to lie still on the sea bed. It worked and eventually the sharks swam away leaving them shocked but alive. I give Trev a hair cut but this time I cut it right down to the wood; he gets his own back by cutting mine and leaving it in stripes. I go off to the internet café again and meet an American dentist's wife who has heard a lot about me. She gives me her address so that I can send her a copy of the book I've told her I am writing; I might even take it to her myself.

Collecting Marina who is waiting on the shore this evening I tell her point blank, "I'm in the mood" and that she is the only one around.

'And me too, old lad,' she says.

We stay rather late before returning to *Antinea* but keep it a firm secret.

Next morning when I take the rubbish to the skip on the village jetty, Marina comes along,

'Do you know I'm feeling really good after yesterday?' I tell her she's not the only one.

Trev wants to check the current in the passé using the hand-held GPS; I take him along in the dinghy and by letting it drift we find the flow is down to 5 knots so we prepare to leave. We take the anchor up around 1130 hours and by now the current has slowed down to a little over 2 knots so we have an easy time getting through and are soon under sail again doing 9 knots.

Chapter 11

Tahiti

We are heading for Tahiti where it will be goodbye Sue. We'll also be booking our flights to England for the middle of June. At 1400 hours we catch a three foot barracuda; there is no food left on *Da Capo* so they come alongside and we throw them a lump of the fish over. We've put in a way-point for Papeete and find that around 1130 hours we will be passing close to a small atoll. That means taking extra care with the navigating to ensure we don't end up like Robinson Crusoe. We are joined at dinner by the fish we caught earlier, magnificently prepared by our lovely French chef then we wash it down with gin and tonics followed by a bottle of red wine.

The night is so cold that I have to wear a sweater; the wind has gone onto the nose and we are hoping for a change overnight. Instead it drops off altogether forcing us to motor. When I wake up Ady has caught a 40lb dorado and he comes alongside to throw us a massive piece.

Our first sighting of Tahiti is from eighty miles away and honestly you can actually make the island out even at this distance. Beer o'clock isn't until 1300 hours when *Da Capo* comes alongside again to remind us and to cadge a couple of cans. The day passes uneventfully but we have to motor sail all the time and when we drop the main after dark I find the bow light won't work so we have to use the tricolour instead. Then out of the blue fate strikes us a savage blow; we have finally run out of gin.

We arrive off Tahiti at 1800 hours on the 30th May; it's a momentous occasion for me and the way Marina clings to me, it is for her too; I feel extremely privileged to be here. We are all awake at 0630 hours next morning and after breakfast row ashore to the town. As there is no one in immigration we take the opportunity to book our flights home for the 16th June. We are to fly business class on New Zealand Airlines; the reason for our seeming extravagance is that it is cheaper than BA's economy class.

Tahiti is a beautiful place with lots to offer. There's a choice of quiet or lively bars, beautiful sands, and plenty of good restaurants. Cruise liners visit here so there's always a mixture of tourists and locals and the locals seem to be very nice people. Of course at one time the islanders were cannibals. But I think they've evolved since then – well, I hope so.

We have a look around and call for a beer leaving Marina to stay behind in town. She arrives back after dark at 1630 hours and by that time Trev and me are getting a bit worried. I hear as she calls me from the shore and pick her up in the dinghy. She tells me that Trev is getting quite cold towards her of late but I keep the reason for his frostiness towards her to myself.

Later that evening I take her back into town as she is to join some friends from a boat she sailed on earlier. She has treated herself to a new dress and looks an absolute stunner. I give her the hand-held VHF to call me from ashore when she's ready to return. She informs us that according to local law we are obliged to check out of Tahiti when we leave otherwise we will get big problems when we try to fly or even sail out of the area.

I catch sight of Ady next day as he is just about to ferry Sue across; I quickly jump into our dinghy and go to the local supermarket to clear off and avoid having to speak to Sue. The visit doesn't go down well as they won't sell me any beer due to some stupid weekend law, but I do get a few fresh groceries.

It appears to be regatta day as dozens of canoes built in the style of the old outrigger war canoes are racing for hours around the bay. We regularly see crews practising for hours at every dawn and dusk, the coolest times of day.

After dropping Marina in town Trev and me wander off for a beer but it costs £2.50 for a glass so we tell them to stuff it. We visit the market and find mediocre black pearls selling for $200 each; Trev bought about 400 on Manihi for a few whiskeys and two cheap bottles of rum that only cost him $2.5 each. We return to the boat for several rum and cokes. Ady calls us to say that an interesting lady will be visiting their boat later in the day and would we join them. We say no at the time but later we do accept the invitation. It is just another ruse to palm Sue off. I get fairly drunk but I did manage to leave without her.

Having made prior arrangements to wait up and collect Marina from the shore, I feel really ashamed when she comes to my cabin and shakes me awake; she shouted at me for two hours until some locals saw her plight and brought her back, yet she just smiles and says,

'Don't worry, I am all right.' Trev has lost another pair of specs overnight and isn't in the best of moods. I take Marina to call and see Sue as we are going to town but she latches onto Marina and comes along with us. She is gobbing off as usual so when the girls are looking the other way Trev and I disappear into the throng. It's Sunday and everywhere is closed so we mope around town for an hour then return to the boat. Sitting in the cockpit the only sounds are of worshippers at church. For several hours there is quite a cacophony as various congregations attempt to outdo each other with their vocal renderings but suddenly for some unknown reason, or maybe it is due to divine intervention by a confused creator, all the voices strike one accord.

The result is unforgettable as they sing the Hallelujah Chorus in unison; the effect is enhanced by the semi-circular shape of the bay and the unequal distances of the various churches from the boat. This creates an inadvertent stereophonic effect complete with descant. It is absolutely beautiful and I am fortunate enough to hear it twice more that day sung at different services.

Sunday evening Marina and Lucy go with Sue for a last night out. Trev and I take off to try and find a bar; instead we find a street full of bars and go on the binge. I am very surprised when Ady walks in on us, as he and Trev have been quite distant of late; we have a brilliant night. Ady leads us down the street to a bar full of beautiful women; it is all very different and I am getting a bit excited. During the evening I am approached by a woman who takes me to see two girls outside. I make arrangements with Ady and Trev who say they will wait for me up the street and I am given the pick of the girls for $50 a go.

I do a bit of bartering and get the price reduced to $25 but it seems too easy; I need to be cautious. I face the one I fancy and grab her tits; there's nothing wrong with these. But being wary I take another grab at her crotch and find that I am holding meat and two veg. I set off at a gallop and they all chase me up the street. When I get back to Trev and Ady, they have watched it all and are both rolling with laughter. Ady has a volume of the Lonely Planet, which gives every bit of information about places in the world. In Tahiti, it says, this street is full of beautiful girls but also points out that you won't find a single female amongst them; it has been a well planned set up.

In the South Sea Islands it has long been a custom to rear lady-boys. If a family is without girls then one of the boys is dressed and reared as a girl. This is with the intention of the parents having someone to care for them in old age. On reaching eighteen years old they are given a choice to revert to being a boy or stay as they are; most stay as they are. The easy way to tell them from the real thing is that **1.** They are *always* slim and beautiful, **2.** They have man-size feet. **3.** Do like me and do the easy way - give them a quick grope.

It looks really odd when watching a football or basketball match with nearly a full team of lads and two or three lady-boys who play in mini skirts.

I sleep like a log that night until I am aroused by Marina the next morning; she is sitting on the bunk playing with my toes and explaining that we have a busy day before us. After clearing immigration, we go to pick up some up groceries, wine and beer but Trev throws a sudden wobbly. Marina has only said,

'Sue is about to leave and it will be our last chance to see her.'

Trev is adamant in his refusal to go and gives Marina a bollocking over something and nothing. She is so upset that the daft little thing goes and leaves her passport with a store guard as security for a shopping trolley because she hasn't a coin for the deposit. Not knowing this I empty the trolley and return it to the store while she is seeing Sue off. When she returns she gets me to one side and bursting into tears tells me about the passport.

'What am I to do? she begs. 'There is no trolley to return.'

I tell her not to worry but to go ashore with me; we go to

the trolley park and I put a coin into the first one I see. We take it to the store guard who promptly returns her passport. On the way back she says,

'Don't rush, Arthur, I have somesing to tell you.' Then she goes on, 'I have never met anyone like you, whenever anything goes wrong you never worry and I like you very much.'

She throws her arms around me and is just giving me a big kiss when Ady and Lucy come round the corner; our secret is out. I wonder if they will put an end to it all by telling Trev but if they do he never lets it show and from then on Marina and I are very close.

After lunch we set sail for the island of Mooarea keeping a good speed by motoring with the headsail out. Ady leaves an hour later so we don't see him until he is coming through the passé. When we arrive we find that the passé is at a very acute angle through the reef. It is still scary even though it is well buoyed as it is only about forty feet wide and due to the angle we have to avoid turbulence at each side created by massive waves breaking on the reef as we sail between them. However it is not a problem if you keep your head.

We anchor in Captain Cook's Bay; it is so beautiful. The bay was actually filmed and used as a back drop in the film 'South Pacific'. The first dawn is outstanding as morning mist lifts slowly off the mountains; I feel great as I sip my coffee and plan the day with Marina. A visit to the village is our first job with e-mails to check and answer. Trev has gone off with Ady so I take Marina in the dinghy and keep a watch while she swims over the coral but when she comes back, she calls,

'Come on, mate, now it's your turn.'

She carefully outlines the art of snorkelling and after my tuition I take to the water; it is fantastic, the coral is lovely and lots of fish can be seen. It is the best I have ever done and she follows me around in the dinghy until she is satisfied that I am competent. She drops the grapnel anchor and joins me in the water swimming and playing together with me for quite some time. It is a wonderful new experience. Later, to show my gratitude, I teach Marina how to replace filters on the water-maker and lots of other things on the boat but Trev is in a foul mood again. He tells her that she must never touch anything on her own on his boat. She is quite upset as he won't listen when we try to explain that I only intended to let her learn as she forever wants to extend her knowledge. It comes as a relief when Ady and Lucy join us for drinks as it breaks a lot of ice. We have several bottles of wine followed by rum and coke followed by a bloody good sleep. It rains overnight and once again Trev's bed gets saturated through a porthole he has forgotten to close. We hire two scooters using Marina's driving licence to get ours and she rides behind me throughout the tour. I am a little shaky at first but I don't let her know that it is forty-two years since I last rode on one. We go all around the island and I get back in full swing; we decide to go up into the mountains, which is against the hire firm's instructions. The route we take is up a badly rutted track about eight miles long; I have to steer all over the place to avoid deep ruts and holes. When we arrive at Belvedere, French for good view Marina is like an old woman walking around, her legs are so stiff. She is so scared by it she hitches a lift back by car.

'I am not blaming you,' she explains. 'You are a good rider and I am feeling safe; we will ride again.'

The trouble is that her brother almost lost his life in a motor bike accident and this ride has brought it all back to her. Plus of course she has been warned by the doctors about her circulation. Trev and I race the bikes back; it is quite a good laugh but we have to hose the bikes down before we dare to return them. I meet Marina back at the dinghy dock and tell her that all my friends would be envious of me; here in the South Pacific with a gorgeous little frog for a friend. She laughs and replies.

'Me too, lad, but here I am stuck with a bloody crazy rost biff.' Next day is very hot but it looks like raining; we all go to the internet café and supermarket. Trev's wife rings to say that there isn't a flight back here on the 19th July but we can return on the 24th which is okay by me. Later we find that our flights to Tahiti are booked on the wrong day and that we haven't booked returns. We both leave in the dinghy to put things right at the local airport. It is a nine-mile trip through open sea and we get a right bashing as the sea is very choppy. The boat passé through the reef is no problem but once through Trev takes a short cut through the coral heads; I feel just like a ball on a pinball table as we bounce from rock to rock. Finally we beach and leave the dinghy while we take a three-mile walk for the rest of the way. Everything goes to plan at the airport booking office and we are soon back at the dinghy. However as we wade out into deep water I am suddenly aware of two large eyes sticking out of the water and about to cross our path; the eyes are almost three feet apart. It turns out to be a giant manta ray; I've heard they are harmless but we still keep clear until it has gone on its way.

At first we motor along behind the reef but when it gets dark we go back into the open sea where there is a bit more space; it is to be the bumpiest ride ever and I am glad when we get back to the boat. By then it is time to prepare for leaving; Marina has been a little under the weather of late mainly due I imagine, to being a sort of pig in the middle with Sue and *Da Capo*. While we've been away she's taken a good long rest and is now feeling much better.

A lot of the lights marking a channel through the passé are not working; we have to sail through with a great deal of caution but once we are out in the open sea it is easy going. I stay up for an hour and half with Marina on her watch for a cosy chat about the future. She tells me she once thought of leaving at New Zealand but now she is not so sure; I give her a cuddle as she snuggles up close telling me that she feels so happy and safe. My own watch is 0400 to 0700 hours, by which time I can see our destination.

On arrival at our way-point the passé looks really dangerous but we carefully line up the transits and go for it. There are massive breakers at each side of us so to broach that could well prove fatal but once again we are safely through and anchor up.

The place is quite nice when we go ashore to explore but it is also very hot; a cold beer and a sleep seem the better option after which, we go snorkelling amongst the coral heads. I love it here where hundreds of multi-coloured fish can be seen. Trev meets a barracuda swimming near the surface; afterwards he tells us it lay inches from his face staring at him and all this was a reminder of his last experience with one. I am much better at snorkelling by now; I used to have trouble with water getting down the air pipe but not anymore. It rains so heavily this evening we have an early night; I don't rise too early but when I do there is a strong offshore wind and we are banging on the anchor; overnight we actually dragged it about ten metres. Trev and Ady have gone diving leaving Marina and me to fend for ourselves.

We take our rubbish to a skip on the jetty and look around the village until we find a scooter hire shop where we hire one for tomorrow. Marina goes snorkelling when we return to *Antinea* while I wash my laundry and keep a close eye on her. When she comes in she says, 'It's your turn now, come on, lad.'

She takes me over the coral following around with the dinghy again; I enjoy myself very much, but this time there is a very strong current so we take it in turns to follow with the dinghy. When we've had enough we book in at the gendarmerie where we are told to be careful at night as the locals watch to see from which boat the dinghies come ashore and rob from the yachts whilst the crews are away. We are surprised at this as the locals so far have mainly been honest. Trev is so tired when he comes back that he goes to bed for a sleep. He says he was watched and followed by a large shark for about half an hour but couldn't get away; he was really scared.

Marina puts on a big smile and works her hands like pedals; I ask what she is trying to tell me. It turns out to be that while we were at the scooter hire this morning she ordered two bicycles for later.

'I knew you'd want to go.'

Our chosen route is to be a circuit of the main island; Iles Huahine is made up of two islands joined by a bridge, with both islands locked inside a circular reef; we are to go round the largest island today. I have seen Marina talking to the couple who own the shop and notice that they are both giving me the once over. When we've gone a couple of miles she takes it on herself to advise me how to tackle the strenuous journey. She has been told that there is a very high mountain on the way round and there will be no way that I would be capable of cycling over it.

'But it's no bother,' she says. 'I'll keep stopping while you walk up.'

'Like fuck you will,' I tell her.

On the way round the island we come across a historical site, which includes a full size reproduction of a village community centre and there we meet the curator, a very sexy lady. She is plump like the rest of the local women but speaks with an American accent. As we are the only visitors present she begins to show us around; out of the blue and completely ignoring the fact that Marina is with me, she takes me aside.

'Follow me, I would like to show you something romantic.'

She leads me outside to a platform overlooking a lake and where the scenery really is beautiful.

'Doesn't it make you feel romantic?' she asks.

I reply that it does indeed and instantly she says,

'That's my home over there in the trees; I'll be in on my own tonight.'

When I tell Marina she doesn't believe me, 'You bugger; you tell me anything,' she says.

But the lady comes to us again, making out that she is explaining local cultural habits which must be nothing more than constant shagging. She tells us that she has heard me using several words that appear to have different meanings and goes on to say that they too use words of various meanings. Putea, for instance, which is the name for the type of building we are in but also has a sexual meaning that she will relate to me later. Another word, Ua-Hou, is a type of fish and also a sexual term. She then points to the top of her legs and says,

'You Putea and I shout Ua-Hou!'

We are both helpless with laughter as we leave and Marina says it is a good job that she has been there to save me from being ravished.

Our ride takes us to a stream where sacred eels swim in a pool; they were awarded their sacred status by a chief of the island many years ago. All are massive and tame too; when anyone gets close they roll onto their backs to allow their undersides to be tickled.

Eventually we come to the big hill, but it's no mountain; I let her draw away from me then I open up and speed past her carrying on for a long way before getting off to let her catch me up. She tries to ride but can't and has to walk for a while. She is still puffing for breath when she catches me up. She is amazed and asks how I do it. I tell her it's nothing special, I am good at everything. She just smirks and nods her head knowingly.

We continue our ride and after several pleasant stops arrive at the summit, where we sit and take in the scenery. What a ride it is downhill as I let the bike go flat out all the way.

At the bottom I put the bike's nose down a ditch and sit beside it; she finally catches up and thinking I've come a cropper comes running to me. She is very excited.

'I am not to telling that you get what you ask for, but I will not.'

'Whatever you have said, Marina, sounds very sweet;'

She replies, 'Oh, you crazy, mmm...' She is lost for words for quite some time.

We finish our ride and re-join the boat then we all go for a night out altogether; we have a great meal and several bottles of wine. Back on board we have a fantastic finish to a wonderful day.

When I wake up at 0630 hours Marina is still out sparkers; I have already had breakfast when she wakes up. Trev is in one of his short tempered moods, which lasts for most of the day. He goes off diving again with Ady and Lucy leaving Marina and me alone; she tells me again how happy she is of late and loving every minute.

'Let's go snorkelling again, but together this time.'

We anchor the dinghy while we swim; the current is unusually strong today but we still have a wonderful time. Then we move to a more settled spot and play about for a while until she suggests that I take the dinghy while she swims against the current back to the boat. I can see it is hard going and keep close to her just in case but she won't let me help. When we do get back, she makes another of her announcements.

'Now, marathon man; you have seen I am a marathon woman. Marathon swimmer, now let's go sleep.'

She has prepared a meal earlier and after we have eaten we are both so tired that we go back to bed and sleep until it is nearly time for the others to return from diving. We were going to get the bikes again but decide to have dinner and an early night instead. I get to thinking,

"What if I am doing a silly thing going home when life is so good?"

I sit around again the next morning just gazing into the water, and watching the many fish; it may sound boring but life on the boat is so relaxing that time has no meaning.

Trev comes with us today so we opt for motor bikes and take him to see the sexy curator; she is soon up to her tricks again. There is a picture of a range of hills in the museum; she tells us this is worshipped as the goddess of fertility then goes on to explain why. Sure enough we can see when it is pointed out to us that the range is the perfect shape of a reclining pregnant woman. But our sexy friend needs to go into more detail; she goes through all the facial features, then the breasts and gives us a demonstration at the same time. The belly comes next then at the top of the legs is a copse of bushes that give the area a more authentic appearance.

'Can you tell me what that is?' she asks. No one speaks.

'Well, Okay then just for now, I'll call it her pecker, Ua Hoa!'

We carry on with our tour to a restaurant for lunch and a few beers then we visit the Garden of Eden, a very large area of botanical gardens. After a steep ascent to the top of a high hill we get a panoramic view of the island; however the place is so humid it is nice to get back to the boat for some cold beers. The bike that Trev has been given has no brakes so he has to walk it down all the hills and is definitely not amused.

When we reach the diving platform back at the boat, Trev loses one of his shoes in the water; he dives straight in and is immediately swept away by the strong current. I quickly tie extra ropes onto the dinghy painter, just as I did for Pete in Panama, while Marina plays it out till it almost reaches him; even then it takes a great effort to get to it. We pull him in while he hangs on to it but he has to stand on the boarding ladder for quite a while to recover before climbing aboard. Later we go ashore and have another great night out. When I wake up Trev is still out cold; Marina tells me that we created hell when we came back from town. Everyone had a right bust up including Ady and Lucy.

We take up the hook and sail on again anchoring in another bay for about half an hour. I never find out why apart from letting *Da Capo* leave us.

Marina is very subdued this morning and it takes quite a while before she is back at ease. Our final target, the Isla Raiatea, is now only twenty miles away and that's where we head next.

When we leave for home, a friend of Marina's from another boat is coming to stay with her until we return. I met him earlier and thought it a good idea; at least the girls would not be alone while we are away. She was a little excited to see him at the time but he showed little or no response. I'm sure Trev must have said something to her the night before, but she hangs her head and declines to say anything about the argument when I ask.

Instead of going straight into the marina we sail to Taha, an island just north of Raiatea but still within the same reef. We sail around for an hour and a half, even striking the bottom before we find a suitable anchorage. I suppose we've had a good day but it doesn't seem like it to me.

Marina's English has been improving and now everything is either fucking brilliant or okay mate. But suddenly I am seeing a change in her; she seems to have put up a few barriers. It's as though she is trying to close her mind to something. She holds onto me very tightly every time we are alone and is always reluctant to let go. Whenever I ask if anything is wrong she holds me closer but never speaks out.

The next day we tie up in Raiatea. I do a lot of sleeping and not much drinking then go to bed early. We get some rain overnight; the dawn is lovely and cool even when the sun is high. We are expecting problems getting the anchor up as we are in eighty feet of water but it comes up with little or no effort.

Ady calls and tells us he is in a different marina from the one we originally chose. It turns out to be a good choice and is half the price of the other. We get a bit of bother with the shore power during which Trev gets very frustrated and blows his top. It is a problem no one could have foreseen and is soon remedied but both of us and Marina in particular, get a severe tongue lashing. I give her a reassuring hug as she appears to have really taken it to heart.

Only three days to go then I'll be home to see the family. We have a wonderful night, Marina has made more fancy crepes, but later gives me devastating news. She will have to move on when we return from England. She puts her arms round me and weeps for a while then asks me to always keep in touch with her.

Most of our time is spent finishing outstanding jobs on the boat and preparing for home; once again I am off my eating and feeling out of sorts, maybe due to the excitement of leaving. We three plan a final get together in town and are joined by Ady and Lucy. It is indeed an excellent night out with the restaurant proprietor giving us all a lift back to the marina where we finish the night off with Chivas Regal.

Marina organises a taxi to the airport for us then after one of her wonderful cuddles I have to leave.

Chapter 12

Flight to England for R & R

The flight to Tahiti is late so we have a few beers to keep cool. We have a further four hours to kill in Papetee, which we pass over a meal and a lot of ale. Then in the airport VIP lounge we are given as many G &Ts as we can drink and all the way to England we are treated to champagne and wine; what a trip. Travelling Business Class is given the thumbs up. We cover 12,500 miles landing in London at 1030 hours and by only 1200 hours I am on the last leg, on the train heading for Scarborough.

To my delight my son Kevin, my daughter-in-law Tracey, and granddaughter Jessica come up to see me the day I land home. I tell them all I can about my adventures in the time we have. The next day, Saturday, I take a trip to Batley to visit my brothers and am pleasantly surprised to find a car waiting for me to view. A customer at our garage wanted to sell it cheap to one of us and my brothers knew it would be very suitable for my needs. I immediately buy it as they have judged right.

Everyone is more than excited to see me and hear about my voyage but a day is not long enough to tell them everything. I have to return to Scarborough tonight and when I have been back in my flat for only a few hours the reality of being alone is a most unwelcome feeling. I miss not having my wife Iris with me and it is worse than ever seeing little reminders of our long marriage together. Photographs and the like haunt me. I still do have my friends, of course, but I find that after the pub closes I am back in lonely mode alone with my thoughts and memories.

Trev pays me a visit one weekend and we have a night out together but all too soon it is over and he leaves. One thing that cheers me up is the receipt of an e-mail from Marina saying she will wait for me to return before leaving the boat. At least I have this short reunion to look forward to.

Most of the five weeks I stay in England is hum-drum as my sons and families have their own lives to get on with so I am unable to see much of them. I am actually pleased when it is time to go back to Tahiti.

On the day I am due to fly I have amassed so many spare parts for *Antinea* that my baggage weighs sixty-five kilos. The new back pack I've bought breaks before I even leave Scarborough railway station. On the short journey to York I am hard-pressed to repair it with strong needle and thread that of course I carry. At York station where a footbridge has to be crossed carrying your own luggage; a kind fellow passenger helps to take the weight of my backpack as I mount the stairs.

My first opportunity to sit back and relax doesn't come until after baggage check-in at Heathrow where Trev joins me in the VIP lounge. Gin and tonics are top of the menu now. We are able to sleep on the flight to Los Angeles before boarding the plane for Tahiti.

Chapter 13

Return to Paradise

We return to Tahiti on July 25th 02; there isn't much to do until our flight to Raiatea so we down cans of beer until 0630 hours when we are ready to do justice to a full English breakfast. Marina is waiting to meet us at the airport. It is lovely to see her again but I feel very sad as she is to leave quite soon. She gives us both a hug and takes us to the boat in our dinghy.

Antinea is gleaming; she must have spent a lot of time cleaning it up. I am very sorry to see her go. She gives me a big hug and a kiss and asks me once again to keep in touch; then she is gone. I really must admit that a little part of me goes with her.

Trev and me both sleep well in the cockpit then go out for a meal to the same place we had our last one before leaving Raiatea but there is no atmosphere to the evening; it is just not the same anymore.

While reading a magazine we see an editorial saying that everything in the Cook Islands is very expensive; we hire a car and go to stock up with supplies. It turns out that the statement in the magazine is totally wrong; the truth is quite the opposite.

It seems like a good idea when Trev suggests hiring a car. We take a tour of the island and he drives the damn thing so fast there is no chance to take much in. To top it all we arrive back early to spend the rest of our day sitting on the boat.

On Saturday we sign out at the gendarmerie then go to town in the dinghy. I think it a good idea as we are able to check out the fuel dock etc.

Once again we are on our travels; we fill up with fuel and water before motoring out through the passé. Ady has left already and he is to call at Bora Bora, Niue and the Cook islands; it will be a while before we see him again.

Soon we are romping on at 7.5 knots heading for Bora Bora. There is a big rolling swell but the sun is hot; we reach the passé at dusk and by that time night is upon us. We have to negotiate the passé and anchorage in total darkness until we find a suitable depth to drop anchor. After an hour we pick out a group of yachts in the gloom so enabling us to find the bottom nearby to them and after a few beers go to bed.

When breakfast is over we fit a new baby-stay that I had made in Whitby. It is a perfect fit having been manufactured exactly to the measurements I gave. We can now get a bit more shape to the mainsail. I brought a heater motor from a Ford Transit in an English scrap yard and spend an hour adapting it to fit the engine blower. It is a proper struggle fitting it back into the engine area and I am black as the ace of spades when I've finished and have to take another shower.

We move to another anchorage close to the yacht club but due to Sunday laws the club is closed. I repair the windlass wiring by connecting the control cable directly to the solenoids; now it is time for sundowners.

Chapter 14

Rarotonga - Cook Islands

Rarotonga in the Cook Islands next stop; we are away at 0800 hours. It is 400 miles away, or as we say "only to Holland and back". We sail with a thirty-knot wind and a two-metre swell while keeping up a steady speed of 7.5 knots. Together we attempt to pole the Genoa out but it must be in poor condition; it rips right across the foot allowing the blue anti-UV section to fall apart. When we have the sail halfway down we are hit again by 30 knots of wind and have to motor head up to wind to help us with removal of the sail. Even then it is horsework but putting up the new sail is even harder. When it is set and working I find it has actually taken us one and a quarter hours from the time we first released the halyard.

Just imagine what it's like with the bow crashing into the surf every minute and 30 knots of wind trying to tear the seventy-odd foot sail out of your hands. We finally get the boat back on course and are sailing again. With the job done we admit we are both absolutely knackered and I am past eating anything come dinner time. I've just time for a short nap before standing watch where I stay all night until 0530 hours; one hour of sleep and I am up again at 0630 hours. The wind dropped at 2400 hours and we've been motoring ever since; this goes on all day and all night again.

Our day has been uneventful with most of the time being spent reading. I have a tinned mackerel salad for lunch and steak with fried bread fruit for dinner followed by G & Ts before standing watches 2100 to 2400 hours and 0330 to 0630 hours.

We've had a fishing line out for two days; the only bite we have had bent a very large hook, and got away. At 0530 hours when the wind picks up slightly I am able to trim the sails to help the engine a bit until the direction changes and we have to tack.

Conditions become much better overnight; I stand a watch from 0430 hours during which the roller reefing drum gets jammed again and as we are diving into the swell I end up getting totally drenched. A hot shower and change of clothes works wonders though and it's time to catch up on some badly needed sleep.

When I am back in the land of the living again the wind is back up to 29 knots with a three-metre swell running. We are constantly getting soaked and feeling very cold. I am on watch next morning and making coffee when suddenly the main gybes. The auto-helm is displaying a text I don't recognise and not responding; I put the engine on and call for Trev while at the same time putting the helm on manual control. We resume our course but the helm doesn't feel right to me. Trev takes over while I go below decks to check it out; the cables that work the rudder stock have been stretched in the foul weather. By lying down in the narrow space between the cockpit sole and the hull, I manage to adjust them. It is a very difficult task while on the move; you are constantly chasing the adjusters back and forth, while at the same time keeping out of the way of a quadrant that could take off your fingers if given the chance.

Once the adjustments have been made we are able to revert to automatic control; today is particularly hard going as we are constantly beating into winds of over 20 knots. It is sunny but still really cold and the seas are mountainous. We need both sails reefed down to try and slow us down so we can arrive at our destination in daylight. We've been trying to use up all our fresh fruit and vegetables; Rarotonga is a New Zealand controlled island and the MAFF are said to be very fickle about fresh food being taken in. I can understand their reasoning as this way they reduce the risk of crop diseases affecting their own. Trev has already used up all our bananas and dried fruit to make some bread. When dawn breaks the wind is near gale force and we have very mountainous seas but I can just make out the town of Avarua fifteen miles away where the only harbour is situated. As luck would have it a direct course will put the wind right on our nose, so we have to put in long tacks until we get closer to land.

To create the harbour at all must have been quite a feat as most of it had to be blasted out of the reef; there is only one passé and the harbour is tiny but we make it safely without any problems and are soon riding at anchor. Now it is time for a late breakfast and a good rest after which we pay a visit to immigration. The guy who attends to us is a proper gentleman and we are sorted within minutes. He asks about fresh food and we tell him we have eaten everything apart from four apples; he shows us a waste bin and tells us to just sling them in. Being true Yorkshiremen we don't use it; instead we put them in the oven to stew but we fall asleep and burn them. Then we throw them in the bin. We have saved all our vegetables too and Trev makes a nice thick broth with them; we also get away with all our pickles so in the end nothing is confiscated. Both of us have a good long sleep during the afternoon until we are awakened by a call from Ady. He is in the North Cook islands and tries to persuade us to join him there. We have already gone through the charts and found there isn't anywhere deep enough to accept our draft (the depth of the boat that is below water-level). Later this is confirmed when he tells us he touched the bottom and he doesn't draw anything near as much as we do.

We are sitting out on deck when a German boat makes the harbour; immediately the Yanks are swarming around to organise him. There is one guy in particular, on a boat called *Final Straw* who keeps calling him on the VHF to stay well clear as he has a long anchor chain out and he is over it. Everywhere the bloke goes they call on him to move and after a while the German anchors miles away. I would have told the Yanks "bollocks".

I have an amusing night exploring the town; we both get pissed but so what. The beer is only $NZ 7.5 a litre, about £2.50p. I meet a New Zealand estate agent who gives me her phone number to call when I get there; by the time I arrive I have my hands full. A shopping expedition the following day brings a pleasant surprise: the price of food is very much less than in England. Even at an open market where fresh fruit and vegetables are of a very high quality we find it is cheaper too and stock up with supplies. On another tour around town we find 'Trader Jacks', a smashing bar with a balcony looking over the sea. The place was flattened a few years ago during a hurricane but was rebuilt incorporating hurricane-proof safety factors.

We are finding this place to be a quite refreshing change; due to a strong New Zealand influence the town is a lot more up to date than anywhere we've seen for a long time. Dinner is a delicious salad using fresh produce from the market. After eating, just for a change, we have a night out on the town. We do drink a lot of ale and all in all we have a bloody good night.

When we left Raiatea we filled our water tanks but ran out before arriving here; I need an answer as to why. It turns out to be a loose connection on the diving platform shower. The leakage is equivalent to leaving a tap turned on.

I find an internet cafe and contact Marina to see if we are still friends. She replies instantly saying,

'Yes! And you'd better believe it, mate.'

I wake up rather late, which for me is always the sign of having had a bloody good night out. It is festival week here so I am hoping for a long stay. I take another hike up the mast to fit a new set of lazy jacks; these are a simple device designed to keep the mainsail tidy while being lowered. It must be catching because for most of the day we are lazy too, devoting our time to the emptying of beer cans.

Ady calls again asking us to join him up north but no fear; the sea is still rough and he is 140 miles away. One thing I like about being in this place is the absence of damn mosquitoes, but the town virtually closes down on Sundays. To pass the day I change the engine oil again; it's a lousy job as you lose all the dirty oil from the filter into the bottom of the boat and then have to mop it up. The designers have not left a space to put a drip tray under the engine; the boat is French built, giving me an impression that not all frogs are as good as the one I'm used to.

We find a bar that sells fish and chips and mushy peas; it's like all my birthdays have come at once. They are terrific especially when we follow them with a few beers.

A very nice German girl is seeking a position on *Antinea* and we go to meet her; I offer to let her work under me but Trev won't hear of it. I see her many more times at our various ports of call right up to reaching Tonga but Trev is never to change his mind.

Alterations in the weather have been dramatic since leaving

Raiatea; we've only moved 600 miles west yet it has got so cold at night that I have had to use my sleeping bag for the first time.

There is a lively watering hole, Coco's, a bar just over the road from our anchorage. Here we meet a couple from Middlesbrough who are travelling round the world by any means available; they are a young couple about in their thirties, really nice people. At our first meeting we end up at a bar near the airport with them. After this session I awake with a thick head which is unusual for me although it doesn't last too long and after sending out e-mails in town we meet again at Coco's for another binge.

During this outing I also have quite an intimate chat with a local lady who asks my age; I tell her that I am an old man. 'Oh, that means nothing,' she replies. 'I love old men.'

As usual, there is a snag: her husband is the bouncer.

A strong wind warning comes over the air although it won't affect us; we are staying on anyway. There is however a torrential downpour while we are in the bar and as the roof is made from corrugated tin sheets we've a rattling good night by the time the rain stops.

The weather has picked up by this morning and has become quite warm; Trev suggests that we hire a car for two days to see the island. I should have known better; we do a full circuit of the coast road, a trip of thirty-two miles and are back before lunchtime. He drives so fast that we see nothing; however we are able to use the car to collect supplies from a nearby store and transport them back to *Antinea.* The car is more or less stationary from then on as there is nowhere else to go.

The two of us are invited to a crew party at Coco's organised by the Yanks. I meet some nice women who have apparently heard of me over the VHF grapevine; from then on my notoriety becomes legendary and I have many 'brief encounters.' We have found out that duty-free liquor can be purchased very cheaply once we are signed out by customs; this doesn't happen immediately but at least it is something to look forward to.

During our stay here we have a party on board and Trev invites the young couple from Middlesbrough that we met earlier; we have a wild time, but as I am about to climb off the boat to go to Coco's I miss the dinghy and fall in but manage to hang on to the top safety line. I shout for assistance but no one comes; my arms are aching badly by the time the young lad comes to see where I am yet all he does is to say,

'Hang on, I'll be back.' By the time he returns I've slipped down to the bottom line; my fingers can't hold any longer and I drop into the water but grab the dinghy.

Trev appears, shouting, 'Why not climb in the dinghy?'

My response, 'If I had any use left in my arms, I would.'

The two of them now climb in the dinghy and pull me aboard amid several unsavoury remarks from Trev. We have a few more beers and then guess what? Trev falls in the drink.

Another day dawns and it is a busy one for us; I carry out a big fibreglass repair on the cockpit table while Trev dives to replace the prop shaft anode. We are so engrossed in our work that beer o'clock isn't until 1330 hours, a serious error of judgment that gets a mention in the log.

As we are due to leave the next day we check out early then fill up with fuel at 34p a litre; our harbour dues, which include toilet facilities, come to £30 for eight days and our ale bill for four pints £4. Are we getting ripped off in England?

In the evening we meet the same couple again at a bar in town but this time I have a bit of slap and tickle with the girl; at least I do until Trev spits his dummy out and says it is time to leave. This often happens if I get friendly with a female and he doesn't. Not to be awkward at all of course, but I sit up late and drink a bottle of wine; the next day I get up late and wish I had never drunk it.

We go off to get our duty-free supplies and Trev goes daft over the job; he orders 480 bottles of wine. Yes that's right: 480 bottles. I say it is far too many and after a lot of muttering he reduces the order by 120, saying to me, 'If you can't afford to stay, go home.'

I reply that it isn't the cost that worries me but the lack of space; where are we going to store it all? To make things worse he orders a further nine gallons of gin, ninety-six pints of tonic and 240 cans of beer. We end up with two very large loads to shuttle out in the dinghy; and that is the easy bit. All the cardboard cases have to be removed to prevent cockroaches and then the liquor stowed away. It is everywhere! Under the floor boards, packed in lockers; we even have to alter two bunks into shelves and later during storms we sustain many breakages. The bill comes to NZ$5300 at 2.7 to the pound. Ady takes five cases off our hands to help us out but tells Trev it has been a stupid thing to do.

As we are about to leave the harbour we first hoist the main and just as it fills we raise the anchor; we leave the harbour like a bullet for the benefit of the watching Yanks and have the Genoa out before we are through the reef. It is fantastic surfing on the leading-edge of a low front pushed by 20 knots of wind. The wind increases to 25 knots at 0300 hours so we reef both sails and romp away on a beam reach.

Our ETA at the way-point is 1100 hours but on arrival we find that due to an allegedly inaccurate chart our way-point is actually on dry land; it's a good job that we arrive in daylight. We drop the anchor just outside the passé where Ady and Lucy have come out to meet us in the dinghy to have drinks on *Antinea*. I am made aware by their conversation that Marina's long-standing ambition of sailing to New Zealand has been dashed simply because she joined *Antinea* and though this pleases me it does not please everyone.

We are anchored in open sea in 19 knots of wind and the boat is bouncing around like a turd in the Thames but I am determined to stay alert so we will have no problems. Later we go to *Da Capo* and meet two lads from Yugoslavia: Nerriard and Peter. I remember seeing their boat long ago at Ua Pou; they have been sailing a very long time relying on picking up sponsorship to pay their way.

The reunion was very pleasant but while returning to the boat Trev decides to race Ady. They take a short cut over the reef and we hit every rock between us and the boat. When we are getting into the dinghy I catch Trev by the belt just as he is falling into the sea and haul him back on board. He still insists on being in control of the dinghy and becomes very angry when I suggest that he go a bit slower. On our arrival at *Antinea* Ady uses a bit of sense, deciding to stay the night aboard with us rather than risk the passé again in darkness.

Later Lucy takes me aside and says she is sorry how things have turned out over our little frog. She tells me that she was aware we had something going and that while I was away it was quite plain to see Marina was very unhappy though she tried not to let it show.

A new day and we go to eyeball the island; what an experience it is going through the passé. It is only 40ft at the widest point and with a dog leg too; several parts of it are only two metres deep and there is a constant outward flow of 5 knots. We need to put the motor on full throttle to make any headway at all through the outfalls.

I find the island and its people to be extremely nice; while visiting a shop-come-bar I have a couple of beers and a brief chat with a Maori woman. She is getting very hot and excited before we leave; I ask her if she knows why beer was invented. She doesn't, of course, so I let her know it was to help ugly people to have sex.

She laughs and says, 'I would not need any beer if it was to be with you.'

Her sister, who runs the bar, tells me, 'You shouldn't have said that, she'll be on heat for weeks now.'

We find an internet shop but don't bother to stay as the price is a pound a minute due to low demand and high costs from the service supplier.

When I was talking sense to the Maori woman she told me a good story that I think is worth a mention here.

"Sometime in February this year a man went fishing in his motor boat off Papetee; his engine cut out never to run again. The man, who had no flares or VHF with him, ended up drifting around for five months and three weeks living off any fish he caught. This was his main source of food and liquid which he took in by chewing and sucking the raw fish; his only other supply of water was by erecting an oilskin overnight and then licking off any condensation that collected on it. Back in Tahiti he had long since been given up for dead but one day he was washed up on a muto, small islet, here in Aitutaki. He was in very poor health when he was found and in desperate need of hospital treatment. The French government, who own Tahiti, heard of his miraculous escape and wanting to make a big issue of it sent an air force plane to fly him back to Papetee, but he told them.

'I wouldn't fly in a fucking French plane if it was the last one on earth.'

So now he's become a hero in Aitutaki too which is New Zealand owned."

We see several yachts arrive and sail close up to the reef but when they see the passé they have second thoughts and leave.

The island is really beautiful and we want to see more so we hire a motor bike and go for a tour around the whole place. We have arranged to meet Ady and Lucy at a restaurant for lunch; it is situated right out at the end of a peninsular with an excellent view of the atoll and muto's. We decide on making the trip overland, a big mistake. While going up a very steep and narrow track the front wheel becomes airborne; I am thrown off with Trev and the bike falling on top of me. I get a few burns on my legs from the hot exhaust but we have a good laugh. We fall off again before we get back but suffer no damage on this occasion. Back at the dinghy dock we meet a pleasant American couple who we are to meet up with several more times along our voyage.

Ady comes over for the night and we have a real good booze up before bedtime. Morning brings another chore to carry out to the filters on the water-maker. They smell absolutely foul so I change them. There is so much plankton in the sea that it clogs the filters in no time at all and then goes rotten; we find this occurring several more times until we get in cooler water.

After signing out at immigration we make preparations to set sail for Palmaston Atoll; it takes us over half an hour to break out the stern anchor. We finally do it by winching in hard then letting the swell pull us out; it is a Danfoss anchor and one of the tines ends up nearly bent double in the process. Ady is having trouble too and calls us to help him; he also tells us of a severe storm warning and that we could be caught out with no chance of shelter so we decide to return to Rarotonga. I am all for this as I like the place. We leave at 1400 hours and are soon doing 8 knots almost on course; we hope to be there by 0900 hours in the morning but arrive at 1130. We have no end of bother getting anchored up. I think this is due to having too many tasks to do all at once.

On arrival the weather is great and after our tussle with the anchors it is nice to lie back for a breather. We have a casual afternoon spent in Ronnie's Bar. He's a local lad who has been to England and has played rugby for Leeds. It must have been a smart bar at one time but alas by now Ronnie is a full-blown alcoholic and is letting the place go downhill fast.

I check my e-mails but am disappointed as there is nothing new for me so I go back to the boat for another sleep; it is to be short-lived as I am awakened by the sound of a bottle being opened. Trev and me have a couple of G & Ts before going to Coco's bar for even more. I meet a beautiful oriental girl from New Zealand in Coco's and I do my best to get her to come and live with me but the bloke she is sailing with says a definite no. We also meet a Maori man who is a bit of an expert at curing aches. The next day when Trev wakes up he says,

'I could use the Maori guy now. I ache all over but I'd prefer the Chinese girl if I have a choice.'

There are some cargo boats moving around in the harbour; it is quite funny watching on as the Yanks hurl abuse at them for swilling their boats about. I manage to get a few cards off to my friends in England then we go to Coco's Bar again; we no sooner arrive than a drunk turns nasty and tries to crush my hand in a shake. I crush his instead and then make it awkward for him to pick his nose; I flatten it for him. I then turn on the charm with a couple of local girls who turn out to be lesbians and I don't remember much after that.

Saturday 17th August and we rise at 0900 hours only to be told that we will have to leave the harbour to allow two large ships to move about; the harbour is choppy enough but out at sea is even worse. We leave at 1130 hours and put the genoa up to make the ride more stable; then we sail around until the harbour is clear again.

I am just dropping the forward anchor when Trev yells that the engine has blown up. As soon as I see the state of the water around the stern, which has a thick layer of soot floating on the surface, I have a good idea what the fault is but for the moment there is a need to panic. Trev always does things at high speed and right now we are heading for one of the cargo ships without brakes. Several lads in dinghies come to our aid and are trying to push our bow round without success so I tell Trev to stop and restart the engine. Within seconds it is working perfectly again; we easily stop the boat's progress and reverse away.

The same thing happens when we have another try with the anchor, but again a stop and start does the trick. When we are moored up I take out the air filter. It is dirty but not bad enough, so I inform Trev that the fault appears to be in the main injector pump and to let it go for now to see what happens. It seems that it was only a speck of dirt jamming either the rack or excess fuel device; it later clears itself and we have no more trouble.

An invitation to a birthday party given for Harvey, an ex-patriot Geordie, arrives; when at the party an American woman I spoke to at the last party in Rangiroa comes to me for a natter but after her husband makes a big fuss and drags her away I leave and go across the road to Coco's bar.

A day later and we have to be out of the harbour again to allow a ship to enter; this is necessary as several yachts have suffered damage in the past. We are all about to re-enter when a schooner arrives and tries to be first in. Ady quickly tells him that he must wait until last when everyone has picked up their moorings.

It's a Sunday again and once more the town has closed down; the wind has turned and is blowing from the east just as we were hoping for. The puddle jumpers, as the Yanks are also called, are planning a mass exodus tomorrow but we'll have to wait and see as they only seem to move when there is a month-long forecast of sunshine and no more than 5 knots of wind. Six yachts, actually, and all the others make a mad rush to moor on the wall, places that for some reason the Yanks see as a status symbol; stupid from a seaman's point of view as they get bounced backwards and forwards on the surge. It's a vulnerable anchorage anyhow as wrongdoers can simply climb on and off the craft and do whatever bad deeds they've a mind to.

I receive another e-mail from Coral who writes that she hasn't returned to *Antinea* as planned as she could never go back to Trev after being with me. She adds that she would like to meet up with me again sometime in the future

Today I manage to complete a task that has plagued me since the 22nd April, the night so long ago that our spinnaker halyard broke when most of it dropped inside our mast becoming tangled with other halyards and fittings. Ever since then I have given it a light tug in the hope of drawing out a little more rope. Imagine my surprise when the whole length comes free. We can now refit it and have use of an extra working halyard.

While we're having dinner in town Ady drops a real stunner. He tells us that he is thinking about splitting up from his wife and starting a family with Lucy. I've met his family and they think the world of him. Both Trev and I think it will be a real shame if he does but who are we to interfere?

I get quite a laugh when I wake up in the morning. Another boat has arrived and Trev is out in the R.I.B. helping them to moor it up. He takes out the stern anchor in the dingy and drops it well away from their boat but instead of the girl on the boat tying the other end to a cleat, she throws it in the water and the bloke with her has to dive for it. When I meet her later I decide that I would have given owt to go diving for her for she is a Chinese cracker. We are told that she used to work as a pavement masseuse and I put my name down for an instant govey job (moonlighting).

The couple join us on *Antinea* later on that evening together with Ady and Lucy. The next morning Trev and I find dirty plates and pans in our sink but the daft thing is that neither of us can remember eating, never mind cooking. Winnie, the Chinese girl, calls us early to say she is making breakfast and sending it to our boat; the meal when it arrives is peanuts in rice balls. Some people have to live frugally but fortunately we are able to finish off with bacon and eggs.

Trev goes ashore to get a haircut leaving me to sign us out at immigration; upon my return to *Antinea* I see that a new Yank has moored close beside us even though the harbour is half empty. When his boat drifts into us he shouts out,

'It looks as though one of us will have to move,

'Yes, and make it fucking snappy, mate,' I shout back.

Chapter 15

Palmaston the Eeh Bah Gum Island

We leave at 1630 hours after persuading Ady to take another five cases of wine off our hands. Our destination is Palmaston, 266 miles away. There isn't much wind so we have to motor sail but occasionally are able to knock off the engine. It is a miserable night with continuous drizzle but by 0830 hours next morning we have the Genoa poled out and the engine off.

After fishing for an hour we land a ten pound Dorado, our first fish in four weeks. The wind rises to 26 knots and at times we are reaching a speed of 10 knots but as the seas are up to two metres we are getting a very lumpy ride. It is so cold that we both need to wear our sweaters and thick coats; my first time ever on this trip.

By 1430 hours we have broken out the rum for sundowners; it is far too early but there is no sun so we need to keep warm. At 1700 hours our speed is in excess of 10 knots with 36 knots of wind so a reef in each sail is required. The sail becomes more comfortable and we are still achieving 8 knots. Our dinner is very fresh dorado after which I stand watch 2400 until 0600 hours. It is a wild moonlit night and I thoroughly enjoy every minute of my watch. On reaching Palmaston Atoll we find a welcoming party of local lads awaiting us. They point out a safe place to drop our anchor and join us on board for beers. They are three great lads, pleasant to talk to and turn out to be always very helpful during our stay. We ourselves drink a few cans but the lads are putting them away as though it is their last day on earth. When finally their thirsts are sated they leave for shore after saying they will return as soon as we are ready, whatever that means.

We both take a hot shower followed by a nice long sleep. Within a few minutes of a call on the VHF Jimmy is here alongside with his motor boat. He is a massive lad, maybe weighing 158 to 160 kilos and is so fat that he has a job to walk around but he is a really nice lad to talk to. He uses his boat as a free ferry between the island and the anchorage so for that reason we are joined by another couple from the yacht *Poet's Place* to be ferried ashore.

The passé is an absolute nightmare but Jimmy knows it well; he lands us then we are shown around the village, or I should say, *their* part of the village. We are taken to the nice school, so called because the old one had not been very nice. We are introduced to the school principal, headmaster, teacher, you name it and he is it.

I'd better start at the beginning and explain to you about these islanders; I warn you it's a bit of long tale but here goes. In the early 1800s a Yorkshireman set out on a whaling ship and during the voyage became acquainted with an Asian Indian. After visiting these islands they decided to stay. Their ultimate plan was to set themselves up in the business of catching whales and make a living at it, but first their needs had to be met. They sailed to Penrhyn, an atoll away to the north-east where they were to pick up some brides. The Yorkshire man, William Masters did very well; he ended up with three brides while his friend settled for just one. They returned to Palmaston and seemingly were as successful in their whaling as they were in their breeding. So it was agreed that the Indian should travel to New Zealand and set up an outlet for their products.

He must have been away for quite a while, because on his return his wife had two little surprises for him that she could only have conceived in his absence. The children she had borne had been fathered by his 'friend' William Masters. Thus began the first of many feuds.

From then on the island's population has increased to well over fifty, all very proud of their great ancestor, and even today the promiscuous young ladies keep Yorkshire traditions alive.

The islanders even speak proper Queen's English just like ar do. One lass said,

'Dus thar naw lad, thar't fust bloke at's cum here at wi can unda stand?'

Now back to where I was before I gave you the history lesson. There are two female government officials on the island who represent the islanders in parliament at Rarotonga. They are both called masters of course and shag like rattlesnakes. One is in charge of education, while the younger is the Minister for Foreign Affairs. The one in charge of education has met an English barman in Rarotonga and is very impressed with him. So much so that she persuades him to leave his humble job and be elevated to the dizzy heights of School Principal, Headmaster, and Teacher; so there you are, a modern history lesson or just a bit of local gossip. See it as you will. We have been invited back to Jimmy's home to meet his family. They already have a barbecue going when we get there; two gorgeous young girls are doing the cooking. We are shown around before being introduced to the headman David; he seems to be a nice chap but time always tells. We have a natter with the family while the meal is being prepared during which it is made clear that we should only visit *this* particular family group and eat at *this* home. I become very wary when I hear this but it seems all right to join in and give it a try. After the meal I take a look around the village and get into conversation with one of the girls who have been doing the barbecue. I ask her name and she replies.

'Darling.'

'Bah gum, lass,' I tell her. 'Tha's sharp.'

'No, lad,' she replies. 'That's mi name.'

I give her some lipsticks for herself and her sister. Minutes later they are back pouting their red lips while I give both pairs a road test.

After dinner all the active ones meet outside for a game of netball. Every few games two players are changed so that everyone gets a go; rather like on Takaroa, the island of more girls than men. Anyway at the next change I join the game and stand right in the centre close to the net. I am waiting for the game to restart but find everyone staring at me until a big girl playing in our team shouts to another one stood behind me.

'Thee cum eer, lass, an' let t'dwarf take ower theer.'

I'll never play netball again after that.

Jimmy takes us back to *Antinea* in the dark and he does a fair job too; we can't see a thing but he gets us there with no problems. At 0630 hours we are awakened when Lucy calls us on the VHF; they are only five miles away so we prepare for their arrival. Jimmy must have heard the call too as he comes alongside for a beer until they arrive at 0800 hours.

He points out a suitable place to anchor then takes us all except Ady, who gets his head down for a rest, back to the village; Ady misses a good outing.

We are to take part in a bird hunt on one of the mutos; but first we call at yet another muto on which is a little straw hut set just back from the beach. We are met by a young Danish couple who are staying there on a sort of trial honeymoon; they are covered with lumps and tell us they've been almost eaten alive by mosquitoes. The girl doesn't seem at all happy with the experience although she's still game enough to accompany us to the breeding area for bosun birds.

The idea is to collect young chicks; they are only a few weeks old but already near the size of a duck. The mother drives them out on their own, occasionally feeding them, while she hatches more eggs. Our task is to collect as many chicks as possible to take them back to Palmaston.

I go off into the thick undergrowth with a young lad; excellent at tracking he is able to guide us back the way we come simply by following broken or crushed blades of grass. Our party only catches a few birds before moving to another muto where we are shown how to find clams under the reef's edges; I am far more successful at this probably because I am taken under the wing of the education secretary who asks me,

'How do you like Palmaston?'

When I tell her I am having a good time she says, 'That's good; did you find someone to stay over with last night?'

On hearing my negative reply, she laughs asking me, 'Why not, are you a sissy?'

Back at the main island which is no more than a mile in diameter a pen has been built and the birds are thrown in. The food system here works like this: everything caught, fish, birds, or anything at all, is shared amongst all the islanders. Each family's share is reliant on the number of dependants they have. There is a near fight to grab the biggest with Jimmy throwing one lad right across the pen. I find myself conscripted into the death squad; Darling asks if I know how to pluck?

'Just give me the chance,' I tell her.

We have about fifty birds to kill and pluck for our meal, while the older women clean them all out then stuff the heads up the bird's arse. I can only assume that this is to keep an eye on things while they are cooking.

The way they do the cooking is quite unique too; first a big wood fire is built up and the flames allowed to die down until only glowing embers remain. The birds are then laid amongst the embers wrapped in banana plant leaves and covered with sand. They are fully cooked when unearthed and taste fine.

While I am working alongside Darling, she asks me.

'Wud tha like ta stop eer wi'us?'

'O aye.'

'Good for thee.' Is her straight-faced reply before she pipes up again, ' what'ud tha du if tha did stop?'

I explain that I'd take six of their most beautiful girls and breed a new dynasty.

'Weel, a can't see owt up wi that - ther's me an ar' lass ti start wi.' Then she asks. 'Ar owd ar' thar onny road?' I hesitatingly tell her my age.

'Sixty four; why theere's nobbut David 'ere owder na thee but a can't see onny problem.'

Trev , who is sitting nearby comments with miserable irony,

'Looks like I'll be seeing you tomorrow.'

He leaves in a huff to let me get on with forming a new tribe. However I only stay with them for dinner and I am back on the boat by 1900 hours for sundowners. There's time to sow my seeds yet.

Sunday comes and the island virtually shuts down for the day; no one is allowed to do anything. Jimmy picks us up and we eat all of the bosun birds for dinner. The two girls are wearing lipstick and a big grin when they come to serve us, but minutes later it has been washed off; even Trev and Ady who have been to bathe are told off when they return without shirts. Headman David is a proper tyrant. After coffee and biscuits Jimmy takes us back to the boat for sundowners before an early to bed close to the day.

I am awakened by the *Tree of Life* calling on the radio; I met them twice before, at Ecuador and The Galapagos. They follow us ashore to the village where they are met and set upon by Bob Masters who is also immigration officer. He sends them back to the boat until he is ready to clear them in. I would never have expected him to act in this way as he always seems to be very laid back.

While I am having a coffee with David he tells me of the Duke's Pool, a very secluded, deep blue lagoon where Prince Phillip took a swim while here on a royal visit. I enjoy a skinny dip in the Duke's Pool; the water is crystal clear and as I'm swimming a massive turtle rises off the sandy bottom heading across towards me. It sort of weighs me up as something, decides I am uninteresting then swims away. I spend about half an hour in the pool and really enjoy it. Water inside the reef is even warmer than the open sea and that alone makes you want to stay in for a longer time.

We are joined at dinner by the *Tree Of Life* crew and I am soon the main topic of conversation when they bring up my antics with Coral in Salinas. My skipper is not amused and asks Ady to take us back in the dinghy. I think we hit every coral head on the way back to the boat.

An overnight downpour wakens Trev and he tells me we've had a storm but the weather is much better by 1030 hours when we go to the village. I take Jimmy's kids for a walk: a girl about four named Lynnia and a lad of three, Nar. They regularly come to sit on my knee whenever I am in the big house and David gets angry with them. It appears that Jimmy's wife left the family and went to live in Rarotonga.

I am sitting on the boat one morning deep in thought about our little frog Marina when Jimmy and his mate come alongside to wait for a yacht coming in from Bora Bora. It is also an excuse to call for a beer. The boat arrives together with three lovely Danish girls and one bloke aboard. Jimmy makes funny gestures as he is about to pass *Antinea* but changes his mind and comes back for another beer. We are sitting quietly when he suddenly speaks.

'Look, footprints.' Almost at once a whale surfaces about

thirty feet away, and what a beauty.

Later we are all on *Da Capo* and I think Trev is trying to kid us on a bit; I thought I had seen some footprints; bubbles rising to the surface above a whale, when Trev shouts out.

'There she blows.' At the time he has a twinkle in his eye.

Suddenly his expression changes to horror; a massive hump back with a calf has surfaced only a few feet away. I can see a great big eye staring at us and try to appear as uninteresting as possible. My ploy must have worked as the whale turns away with its baby following obediently and are eventually lost from view in the darkness. It's been a great sight to see but very scary.

Jimmy tells us that the cold weather will shortly be at an end and we take his word for it. When we next visit David, Trev takes him a few groceries and things that the family may find useful.

During our stay we find out why David goes to all the trouble of being first to meet visitors. His cousin Bill, a bit of an entrepreneur, built a Yacht Club and bar but unfortunately he is a person David doesn't like so he tries to get all the visitors to ignore him. Once Bill opened a shop and as no one had any money he let them have credit, but they didn't settle their accounts even when they did get cash, so consequence is, no shop.

We also hear from some of the relatives that a while ago a rich Scandinavian man bought a ship and gave it to the islanders. It was used to take their fish catches to Rarotonga, however most islanders found they were not getting a decent return for their labours. It turned out that David had organised the cargo to go through a dealer who sent most of the money directly to his account. This fiddle was quickly brought to an abrupt end. Another thing was that partners in the enterprise found they could borrow money from the banks by using the ship as security; but as no one paid off their debts the bank seized possession of the ship.

While we are having breakfast one day a ship comes and anchors nearby to drop off supplies; it has also brought some police officers. It appears that they have been sent to stop further squabbling over a tractor the New Zealand Government has given to the islanders.

One of the families has seized the tractor in retaliation for losing the ship and this has escalated feuding until it is almost out of control. One family is alleged to have been caught about to set fire to a petrol-soaked relative so things were really heating up. It goes to show that things are not always what they seem, even in paradise.

We've already made up our minds to move on but as soon as our anchor breaks free the current sweeps the boat out to sea. While I race to raise the anchor clear of unseen coral heads, the dinghy has to be shipped aboard while we are on the move. *Antinea* is quickly doing 7 knots on a beam reach towards our next stop 285 miles away. We eat fresh lobster for lunch followed by a can of beer; these lobsters sure have plenty of meat on them. The wind drops off in the evening reducing our speed to 5 knots, even under engine power. We eat a great dinner of lamb chops then after dinner the wind picks up just slightly but enough to be sailing again.

Chapter 16

Shark Infested Beveridge Reef

After a hot shower this morning I feel terrific. The sun is up, flat sea and pulling 7 knots; it's absolutely great to be alive. *Da Capo* is out on our starboard beam and keeping up with us, but later they fall back five miles. At 1730 hours we hook a very large barracuda but after our last episode with one we leave it on the line until it frees itself.

One evening, I hear Trev telling his wife that it would be easier if we had an extra crew member; we've already had one of the best going and lost her, but I bite my tongue and keep my thoughts to myself. We are on a heading for Beveridge Reef; it is an absolute must for us to arrive in daylight in order to recognise essential details as there are no mutos and most of the reef is constantly awash. This evening the sea has built up until the swell is level with our boom; we lose contact with Ady overnight but later he catches up with us inside the reef.

We are having a really rough ride the next day and this is making reef spotting a difficult job; at least it is until we spot a broken trawler lying on the reef. After that it is easy to plot our way to the passé, which proves to be an easy one for a change. The colour of water in the lagoon is fantastic, being several shades of blue; we delight in the unique sight of seeing the overhead clouds caught in the water's reflection. Try imagining blue clouds in a grey sky, they are a beautiful sight. Everyone finds it a relief to be here; even though the sea is level with the rim of the reef, the water inside is dead calm.

The wreck we've seen is an American trawler. It is built from glass re-enforced plastic but it is unfortunately broken in two. We find that most of the things of interest have already been taken from it but while looking in a cabin I see a bench seat similar to a sofa. I push my hand down the back and pull out 'A Fistful of Dollars'. Actually they are quarters but add up to many dollars.

Our first wine breakages occur during the day as we are

pumping out the bilges. I know there'll be plenty more so it isn't even funny to hear "it's no problem" from Trev; broken glass plays havoc with pump valves.

When we were in Rarotonga I'd bent a new painter onto the dinghy and I left the old one on too; however, after towing the dinghy 150 miles to Palmaston Trev, for some unknown reason, removed the old painter and re-tied the knot I'd made on the new one. The next morning we discover that our dinghy has gone off on its own; all that's left is the painter tied to a cleat on the boat. Luck is on our side as the sea is calm and visibility superb. I climb onto the boom and after noting the wind direction I spot it bobbing about in the open sea. Taking up the anchor we leave through the passé and catch up with the dinghy a good four miles away. It has been an easy recovery but we both know how very lucky we've been. The motor alone on a dinghy costs over £2,000. One afternoon when Ady is over on *Antinea* we are, par for the course, having a bit of a booze-up and decide to try our hand at fishing. Some time ago Trev baked bread that turned out to be a bit hard on the teeth so we use some for bait. The fish go mad but we don't get a bite; maybe they don't like his bread? We change our bait to chunks of frozen fish; they go mad again but this time they remove the bait from the hooks. After some debate we try smaller pieces of bait and this time we catch some small fish that we then use as live bait. Straightaway we begin hooking 5ft sharks; they are great inconsiderate brutes and become distinctly savage, even making attempts to join us in the cockpit. It was our intention to snorkel and swim in these waters but we decide to move on realising it is far too dangerous.

After breakfast on Monday 2nd of September we leave for Niue, another island protectorate of New Zealand. Our ETA is to be about 0830 hours the following day, however, the seas rise up to four metres and we play safe even to the extent of only downing two sundowners. Trev bakes bread and it is a great success this time. For most of the voyage we are on the second reef in order to slow the boat as we don't want to arrive too early. I'm awake all night apart from a brief half hour or so as the weather is raging wild. Once in the lee of the island it settles down considerably making it possible to motor sail into the anchorage, where with ease, we moor the boat to a float provided by the authorities.

Our first job is to have a clean-up and a long sleep before passing through immigration. When we do pass through immigration it is with far less difficulty than the pilot had predicted.

While ashore we come across an internet cafe that is actually free of charge and I am delighted when I get word from Marina; she is back in France and already missing me and *Antinea*. She still wants to be back at sea and plans going to study for exams to improve her chances of finding a place on a good boat.

There is a beach resort nearby but when we pay a visit, disappointingly, we find it is as dead as a British seaside resort out of season.

As the island is pretty big we hire a motor bike for the week and for once it turns out to be a really good investment. There are lots and lots of beaches to visit where we see some of the loveliest rock pools I've ever come across and all around the coast are fantastic caves to explore. The stalactites and stalagmites are mostly massive giving some idea of their age, which must be many millions of years.

On one occasion we visit Togo; to get there requires a long walk through forest but it is well worth the effort. The reef has been eroded by prevailing winds until the whole area is shaped into razor-sharp pinnacles. The effect is beyond belief although we really have to watch our step as a fall into the deep crevices would almost certainly be fatal.

At one place we come across a cleft in a rock and descend into it down a very long ladder. We meet Karen and Steve, a couple from the yacht *Poet's Place,* a boat we've seen earlier at Palmaston. The chasm is very long and at one point has a natural access to the sea through a tunnel about twenty yards long. Whenever the sea gets rough water is forced into the tunnel to burst out at the other end, much to the alarm of anyone happening to be close by.

We have heavy rain overnight but daybreak brings sunshine compelling us to take to the woods. We have long since decided not to bother with organised tours; it is far more interesting to wander around on our own.

One day we discover another nice spot; having taken a stroll down a track we arrive at a long narrow chasm with a clear blue pool that opens into the sea at its far end. We enjoy swimming here as the water is cool and very refreshing. Later we all take a free mini bus ride to the beach resort; they are holding a fish and chips evening and to our great surprise we have a brilliant time.

Saturday looks promising. They are holding a fayre or fete at a village further up the road so off we go. It is quite quaint and the villagers have put a lot of effort into making it a success. They have made a rather interesting putting green; instead of holes they've painted small rings on the grass. We don't stay long as it is mainly for the benefit of the kids; instead we visit the local prison to buy vegetables. It is an open prison with its own farm that is worked by the inmates to make the place self-sufficient.

In order to let the warders have weekends free, come Friday the prisoners are let out on the loose for two days, reporting back on Monday. This procedure finally leads to a disaster; one violent man, who is let out, attacks and rapes the wife and daughter of a warder. When he finds out the warder whose wife and daughter suffered takes his shot gun and blasts the convict to death; now it is his turn to be locked up. I mention to someone that it is sad for him to be punished as he had only been standing up for his family.

'Never fear,' I was told. 'In Niue justice prevails.'

He was allowed to choose the jury himself and a verdict of not guilty is common knowledge even before the trial.

We have found a bar that is to be our local; it is part of a small hotel complex owned by a New Zealand couple. I find the old bloke interesting to talk to. He tells us all sorts of things regarding the running of the island. The government, he says, is out of touch with current affairs being influenced in their decisions by the many churches. A good law is the one that allows anyone to build a house wherever they want *and* the land is free. The big downside to the place is the lack of commerce, the main reason so many inhabitants leave for New Zealand.

When a family leaves, the home remains in their ownership with no one being allowed to use it, consequently there are dozens of empty houses wherever you look. It seems such a waste as there are many very nice properties amongst them. No one seems really interested in anything; even the shops only open 0900 to 1600 hours with an hour for lunch. I can virtually smell the feeling of apathy everywhere we go.

Sunday 8th September sees the last of several American boats leave but we can hear their banter over the VHF for a long time after; any vacated moorings are quickly taken by new boats arriving. One interesting vessel comes in, a galleon square rigger that Trev and Ady pay a visit to. It is from Czechoslovakia with a crew of lads who are all about twenty-eight years old; their story goes as follows.

They were all looking for adventure after being restricted for so long by their country's politics but were so poor they didn't at first know how to go about it. Then the idea came to build a ship; after pooling their meagre resources they bought a small area in a forest and sought out some cheap, old, but usable equipment to set up a saw mill. They felled trees to make their own planks then they began construction of their ship; the project took over three years to completion. The finished vessel is seventy feet long overall and from a distance looks a very nice job but close up it is a very different picture. The unseasoned timber has warped and due to the lack of funds mild steel fittings were used so there are plenty of rust stains about.

Only two thirds of the original crew remain but the ones who stay are still very keen. Sailing through Panama had been out of the question so they'd brought it round Cape Horn. One lad tells us that he has spent some time in England working as an au pair in Bishop Auckland, but now he is a part owner of the ship and well on the way in his voyage to Auckland, New Zealand.

We detach ourselves from terra firma and set off for The Kingdom of Tonga, a seriously fateful decision on my part. Our voyage is to be about 330 miles and by beer o'clock we are bang on course, doing 7 knots. The relationship between Trev and *Da Capo* is once again at low ebb; Ady calls to say he is heading for the south islands but Trev sets a course for Vavau in the north.

Chapter 17

Vavau, North Cook Islands

We are sailing with fishing tackle out using warps instead of line; suddenly the boat shudders and about fifty metres of warp lashes over our heads. We never do see the fish but I am sure glad that we didn't land it.

I awake the next morning to the start of yet another beautiful day; we are sailing under spinnaker and what a laid back job it is. We do so well that we have to drop the kite simply because we would arrive too early but we still have a great sail.

My elbow is playing up again so I have to use a sail tie as a sling to support my arm and that seems to ease the pain. Ady was due to call us at 1600 hours but we've heard nothing from him.

As we enter the north island group about 0600 hours the sight that meets our eyes is enough to make any sailor fall in love with the place. We are so used to seeing single islands but here there are dozens and mostly surrounded by gleaming white beaches. After edging our way up a half-mile wide channel we enter a large anchorage beside the main town of Neiafu. The waters of the anchorage are shielded on all sides from adverse weather by wooded hills creating a very picturesque setting.

I have always understood that Trev is supposed to be quick off the mark but he meets his match today; the moment we tie up alongside a large commercial dock he is accosted by a local man selling courtesy flags at $30 each. He tells me later that he has also booked us to a Tongan Feast to be held at the bloke's house that very afternoon at a cost of $100 each and he's already paid the man $60 deposit.

To be perfectly honest I don't fancy going; the bloke looks as though he hasn't washed for a month and his wife doesn't look much better, but the main problem is the timing. It is 1315 hours and the party is due to start at 1630 hours during which time we have to leave the dock and get securely anchored. However, we first need to clear customs, immigration, and

MAFF so it's really surprising that Trev has once again jumped straight in with both feet without thinking it over.

Just as I am expecting, all the offices are closed for siesta. We have to wait for them to re-open and plus the fact that they are not too close together, it takes us quite a time to get all our paperwork in order. All in all it is a time-consuming business. We are informed at immigration that by crossing the International Date Line we have actually lost a full day.

The anchorage is a massive area with a depth averaging fifty to sixty metres and is at the time holding at least a hundred yachts. Moorings can be hired quite cheaply; we find one and get tied up but minutes later are told someone else is using the buoy. Trev searches around until he eventually finds a free one; well, it is for a short time only.

At first sight the town appears to be a bit of a dump yet I soon grow to love it. The girls here are truly beautiful; some are a bit wide in the beam maybe but that only leads to a comfortable ride.

We've taken the dinghy ashore to change some currency. By now it is gone 1700 hours; we have missed the party and decide to have one of our own instead as we are in dire need of refreshment. There is a busy bar at the dinghy dock which will serve our needs and that's where we are heading now.

I don't awake until 1030 hours next day. Trev tells me that the guy who held the party has been and brought a box of things that we might have eaten had we been there. He's also made him pay an extra $140 for his trouble; everything in the box is rotten and has all to be thrown away. Tongans are always celebrating something and like to have big feasts in the process. I heard about a Royal Feast given in honour of the king; admission is free to anyone who attends but quite a few Yanks get conned by touts who sell them tickets. It turns out to be a huge banquet; every guest is served with a roast suckling pig and piles of fruit. However protocol doesn't allow anyone to begin eating before the king starts and as soon as he stops the feast ceases.

The king is a very obese bloke who heaps his plate with food then scoffs it like greased lightning and before many have even had time to start; immediately he has finished attendants gather all the food and clear the tables leaving a lot of the Yanks flabbergasted *and* still hungry.

We take a stroll into town but as all the shops are closed we look for somewhere to get a beer. As we walk around we come across a pizza bar overlooking the anchorage. I have a great time dancing and chatting with the girls who work there, particularly one girl, Eseta, who is a beautiful lass.

After leaving the bar we stop off at the Yacht Club before going back to the boat. We are having a quiet beer when a young woman comes and sits beside me; she originates from Carlisle and is the skipper of a massive super-yacht that has just arrived. I say hello and she gives me a peck on the cheek; the next thing I know she has grabbed my hand and thrust it straight up between her legs. Being a naturally shy person I shrink back in amazement; she smiles and apologises then leaves the bar.

I get the usual display of anger when I get back to the boat about how I always spoil the atmosphere everywhere I go when really I always start off as an innocent bystander. It has always been the ladies who have started it.

During the night Trev soon forgets anything that has happened; we are awakened by a loud crash that shakes the boat from stem to stern. Dashing out on deck we find the boat adrift and we've rammed another yacht; it turns out that the free mooring will now be costing Trev $750. We are very lucky and find another buoy even though it is a pitch black night.

Early the next morning Trev visits the other boat and informs the owner he will pay for all the damage once he provides him with a written estimate. There is a bent stanchion, some broken decking and it will also need a new safety line. Peter, the owner, who is a Yank couldn't be nicer about it and over the weeks we get to be friends greeting each other as such wherever we meet up.

Sunday in Tonga is definitely the Sabbath and is always regarded as such. Except for one bar, run by non-observers of religion, which we are quick to find, all businesses are closed. We call in for a beer, and this leads to us joining in a barbecue, and finally drinking to the death. Trev seems to be relenting over Marina and while under the influence admits that she was a nice girl after all; a fact I have known all along.

I find out that the night before I slept in the same room as the king of Tonga's daughter; actually I was well oiled and tired so I lay down and went to sleep on the floor in the Mermaid Bar. Apparently she was sitting at the next table but she was not put out one bit and even gives me a smile the next time she comes in.

We pay a visit to the shops on Monday and also find a cash machine that is very handy for us as the service inside banks here is always so slow. We are both having a good time of late and there seems to be a bit less tension on the boat just now. Trev has arranged to go diving soon then we will probably be moving on again.

Come the evening and we are in the Mermaid, the Yacht Club, when we run into Sue Lane who tells us that she is about to be dumped from another boat she's been sailing on. She says she's put an advertisement for a place on another boat but so far she has been unsuccessful. I take a look at the notice board and can make no wonder that no one has replied. The advert reads, "*Woman seeks lift to New Zealand, but definitely no sex.*"

I meet several eccentric sailors, one of them being a Brazilian lad, Marco; he is sailing single-handed and is a great lad. He mixes in well with everyone until he suddenly sails off into the blue without a word of farewell to anyone. Another of these single-handed sailors who deserves a mention is Peter, a guy from Switzerland. He is seventy-four years old and has crossed the two oceans on a sixteen-foot ketch he designed himself. When he was nearing Panama his mainmast broke and he completed the voyage on mizzen only. His mast was then repaired while he was there waiting for passage through the canal. He has named his boat 'Peter Pan' and his tiny inflatable 'Wendy'. Peter is a very large built man and whenever he sleeps he has to pack everything away as there is only just enough room inside for him to squeeze in and sleep on the cabin sole. The best part of his tale is that he took on a youth hitching a lift from Panama who slept tied out on the deck for most of the voyage. Peter told us the lad would sit right at the front holding onto the main mast; when he was asked why he said it was to be nearer to land. On making their first landfall the lad jumped ship and Peter never saw him again.

Trev has bought a cruising book of Tonga and prepares for a trip around some of the islands. During the next night another yacht breaks its moorings prompting Trev to stay awake on deck for several nights in case we break free again.

The next day starts badly. It's been raining heavily and Trev has to bale out the dinghy before he can go diving. I drop him off ashore and spend some time writing my diary; on his return at 1400 hrs he says he tried for two hours to contact me on the VHF. I check it out; the channel on the radio is not our usual one and he is the only one who has used it today but he won't admit it.

We are made to move once more from our mooring but this time we use our own anchor and chain. Trev tells me that the dive was the worst he's ever been on and he won't be going for another here in Tonga. Time for another visit to the Pizza Bar or "Ifo Ifo" as it is called, meaning "Yummy Yummy". I invite Eseta to join me on the boat to travel to New Zealand then maybe to come back to England with me for a holiday. She already has a passport and agrees to come but I will only believe that when I see it happen. Our night is, as usual, spent getting well-oiled on double rums.

I am wide awake at 0800 hours but Trev is still away to the world. He awakes much later and ready for a move; after buying our supplies we decide that heading for the islands of Nau Papu and Matamaka about three hours away, seems like a good idea.

Chapter 18

The Sound of
Music in the Hills of Nau Papu

To get to the anchorage is a tricky task, there are so many reefs but the weather is perfect and the scenery even better. There are dozens of islets around, each with a white sandy beach; three little lads pay us a visit on the anchorage. They paddle out in a very primitive dugout canoe complete with outrigger. Later on a little girl and two small boys try to sell us sea shells; the girl, who is obviously their spokeswoman, asks for a biro and paper. I give them a biro, a lipstick and three lollipops instead but am forced to smile as she carries on and asks for a magazine, jewellery and a calculator. Trev overhears and shouts,

'Give them nothing, they're all scroungers.'

They understand Trev's *Plane* English and return to their village.

For dinner we have roast chicken legs that Trev bought in Neiafu; they are so tough that I wonder if maybe they've come from an animal that had fur not feathers when it was alive. I've since been told that they came from Australia and are definitely boiling fowls and unsuitable for roasting.

We pay a visit to the nearby village where we meet an old lady who seems to appeal to Trev's maternal instincts as she manages to get $20 out of him for a painting on a piece of bark.

The day following our dinner of tough chicken legs I am sitting out in the cockpit when I hear the sound of beautiful singing. At first I think we've been joined by another vessel as the sound is so clear, but we are still alone. After sweeping the shore with the binoculars I pick out a low lying hillside behind the school where about forty very young girls are getting "All Things Bright and Beautiful" off their chests. The small bay and hillside works wonders with the acoustics and I sit listening for over half an hour to other melodic renditions until it is time for their lessons to begin. It is then that I find the old adage of "there is no accounting for taste" to be so true. The skipper comes on deck to inform me that we will be moving on,

'I don't want waking up again by that bloody racket.'

As we are about to leave a bloke on the shore whistles to us and asks for a lift to an island lying in the line of approach to our next stop. He tells us that it is where he keeps his fishing boat; the water around the island is too shallow for *Antinea* so he has to dive in and swim part of the way.

This evening we pay a visit to the "Pop Ou Beach Resort" on a nearby island. The owner, an Austrian, is the chef and the barman too; talk about chief cook and bottle-washer. There's a steep hill to climb before reaching the restaurant; we are totally knackered and ready for a cold drink by the time we arrive. We actually drink several beers while eating the excellent meal but alas, he keeps plying us with 100% proof schnapps. The next thing I know I am waking up on *Antinea* this morning; the events of last night are a complete blank from the point where we finished eating.

We have the VHF turned on and are suddenly shocked to hear a Mayday call; some guy on the whale-watching boat has been attacked by a shark and is in a serious condition. When several swimmers dived in the sea to join the whales, a shark swam too close for comfort; the Tongan lad kicked out to scare it away but it bit out a piece of his thigh making a real mess of him. We can hear lots of shouting and screaming over the radio but we are too far away to be of any assistance. The outcome is that he lives to tell the tale and is later taken to Australia for further treatment.

Trev tells me that the night before as we were descending the hill I lost my footing and went hurtling past him; in an effort to save myself I grabbed hold of an ornamental tree, which unfortunately snapped off at the roots. Luck was on my side however as the hotel gardener, assuming that I'd damaged my legs, carried me to the beach. Apparently I slept most of the night in the bottom of the dinghy. Trev has no idea how the hell I've managed to get out and on to the boat, nor have I for that matter. I awoke this morning feeling as though I'd been eaten alive; the mosquitoes have taken advantage of me during the night and I can count forty-seven bites on one leg alone. It will take too long to carry on counting so I'm just going to slap on the salve.

We leave the mooring at 1100 hours on headsail only. I go to see my Friendly Island girl on reaching Neiafu but am immediately dragged away to another bar for happy hour where I am joined once again by Sue. I am actually having a sensible chat with her but again we have to rush away "to do jobs on the boat," which then turns out to be reading a book to pass the time.

We are booked to go on a whale watching trip the next day; I am not looking forward to going but how wrong can I be? The tour departed from the Mermaid Bar in a boat built similar to a landing craft. Within half an hour we have sighted our first whale. The skipper approaches it very slowly until we see there are in fact three; two cows - the mother plus a nanny with a young calf. The nanny does exactly the same as a human nanny - helping the mother with her calf. The calf is having the time of its life playing and leaping like all young ones do. It actually broaches completely clear of the water, twisting and turning before slapping back into the water flat on its back. To top it all the mother does exactly the same; what a fantastic sight it is too. Mother whale is tall as a tower block when she leaves the water and when she splashes down it's like a depth charge going off. The time has passed so quickly during all this excitement that when I look at my watch it's already lunchtime.

The boat is driven onto a beach where we have a swim before enjoying a lovely barbecue. Nothing has been spared and everyone is delighted with the meal.

When we go back to sea another mother and calf are sighted but a following yacht and motor cruiser whose crews are inexperienced in whale-watching get too close and the cow becomes angry. We are able to get two lots of swimmers into the water and they manage to swim close to the whales; but eventually enough is enough and the cow starts slapping the water with her tail. It is some sight and it goes on for at least five minutes until they take a zigzag course away from us; the only thing to do now is to return to base. It has been a day that I shall never forget and I thank my lucky stars that I came on the trip.

We have a chat that night and Trev tells that we may be leaving for home (England) towards the end of November.

Once again I awake to a beautiful day; the sun is really hot. I plastered a lot of ointment onto my mosquito bites last night and they are starting to improve. Following a foraging trip ashore we spend a lazy day on the boat. For dinner we have a leg of lamb that is so tough it makes my jaws ache and I guess it's probably sourced from the same place as the chickens. To my delight we then spend a full night in the "Ifo, Ifo". The girls are on top form and we have a lot of fun and laughs with them; I get to know that the three are sisters.

When we awake at 0930 hours I'm feeling fine but Trev has a bad head and as there are a few jobs to catch up with I get stuck in and soon have the boat shipshape again. It's much easier in the long run if the work is kept up to.

An American woman is cutting hair to raise money to help the lad who has been bitten by the shark and I am only too pleased to put my head on the block.

Ady sails in about 1630 hours and suddenly all our plans change, though not for long. The anchor comes up so that we can get nearer to him and we join them for drinks followed by a meal out together. Ady suggests a visit to the "Ifo, Ifo"; I am just starting to enjoy myself when once again there are "important discussions to be held on the boat." The important discussions mooted are merely to tell me that we *may* be moving on soon. I've had a busy morning washing my laundry and bedding but one good thing about being in Tonga is that wet things are soon dry again. We are in the Mermaid bar early this evening and having a good time as Ady and Lucy have joined us; they leave our table after only a short time to go to sit with some Yanks. Trev gets angry over this and I am surprised when he says we will take the dinghy across to the "Ifo, Ifo"; the girls are delighted to see me and we both enjoy the whole night out.

I tell Eseta that we may be leaving soon and ask if she still wants to come with me.

'Yes, of course I do,' she replies.

Eseta only needs time to tell her family and friends; it is looking as though I am not going to be as lonely as I was on my last trip home.

On our way back to the boat Trev is as usual driving the dinghy flat out. Suddenly I look up and see we are on a collision course with a huge catamaran only about ten yards away. I shout a warning but instead of closing the throttle he violently swings the dinghy round throwing me over the side. He doesn't stop as he should do but carries on searching for me; endangering my life further as the night is pitch-black; he could easily run me down or even worse mince me with the propeller.

Luckily I was holding the painter as I went overboard and manage to keep a grasp on it but the speed Trev is going draws me underneath the dinghy; I dare not let go as my feet are trailing in front of the propeller. I manage to force my left arm outwards and this action drags me from under the boat enabling me to shout out. Thankfully Trev hears me and immediately stops the dinghy and pulls me aboard. The cheeky bugger then says,

'Why did you panic and jump?'

I am so grateful that I've been born lucky that I don't bother to answer him.

I have let Ady have my Media cards so that he can download photos from my camera but it turns out to be a failure. It was for Trev too; I think all his pictures were wiped clear. Ady tells me that he called in the bar for breakfast; everyone is excited as Eseta has told them about coming with me to New Zealand and then on to my home in England.

Another short cruise has been arranged; we anchor near Swallows Cave, so named because it is home to a lot of birds. There are some terrific formations in the cavern but they have been defaced by tourists painting graffiti everywhere. Later we are joined by another eight boats including *Da Capo*. The wind gets up overnight but we don't drag anchor; we spend a quiet night discussing my plans to bring Eseta along and I agree with Trev to take full responsibility for her whilst she is on the boat. We are both suffering a bit from upset stomachs then we find that our milk is curdling; it seems that is the cause as once we sort the curdled milk problem out we are soon feeling shipshape again.

Trev takes the inflatable to the beach as it is taking in water and the beach will provide him with a sort of bench where he can repair it and I go along too. I have seen advertisements for a bay where beach parties are held; once at the beach I take a walk through the woods to Turtle Bay. When I find it I have to laugh when I see the primitive facilities for parties; a small square marked out with lines of string and the evidence of past camp fires used for barbecuing the food is all there is there.

While we've been ashore Ady has moved on again without letting us know and once again Trev is seething but I recall many times when he has done the same. I refuse to take sides with him this time when he gets angry by taking a neutral stance.

On the move once again we have 27 knots of wind as we go onto a beat through the many reefs, but in the end we get a place in an exceptionally nice but windy anchorage. There is a hotel on one of the islands and we book a dinner for tonight. After dinner I am happy that we've had a reasonably priced night out and we got a bit of impromptu cabaret thrown in too. It cost us £27 each all-in but Trev insists that we've been ripped off and yet I've seen him literally throw much more than that away many times before.

At 1030 hours next day we set off for a pre-arranged anchorage. On the way I study the chart for access and see that there isn't enough depth of water for our draft; so it's about-turn to where we've only just left and we're having a hard time of it as we have to beat into gale-force winds.

Ady calls up out of the blue asking us to join him again. That turns out to be a good idea.

When we all get together again I receive advice from the two experts on how to make the best of my new-found love life; then I get drunk again.

The anchorage is great, an almost land-locked lagoon surrounded by high hills but the passé is a tight squeeze and very shallow too. It can only be entered at certain states of the tide. There is also a false passé with a wrecked boat that has tried to get through and got stuck high and dry on the reef in the middle; the unwary get no sympathy here.

Not far from the anchorage is a very nice hotel and

restaurant run by a pleasant New Zealand couple; everyone has a good night and a lovely meal and even Trev and Ady kiss and make up; about bloody time too.

Strong winds are forecast making it prudent to stay for a while; there is another island close at hand where Trev and me go in search of some citrus fruits reputed to grow there. After hacking our way through the dense vegetation for an hour or so, we decide it has been a fruitless trip and we settle for a trip to the bar instead.

I am suffering badly from ulcers to my mouth and tongue, which are painful to say the least but I'm hoping some capsules I have with me will help. Ady calls for a natter and we take another trip to the bar for a nightcap, a much better cure for ulcers than capsules. The next day my ulcers are much better making it more comfortable to eat.

During the day we have a visit from an islander who brings two little boys with him in a tiny dugout canoe; they are lovely children and one tot comes to sit on my knee for a cuddle. I give them a lollipop each and their dad exchanges some bone fish hooks for a few trinkets before they leave.

The return sail from Hunga is accomplished with the wind on our nose all the way back to Neiafu and takes four hours; however we do have a little fun on the way. As we sail up the main channel to Neiafu we are following some yanks in a charter boat. The wind is still on the nose but as we are having a good time we aren't really bothered that we need to put a few tacks in. We notice that the charter boat is following our actions and do the same until they are now following our every move so we join in the race too.

We keep up to them for a while and then I sit with my legs over the side. Trev asks what difference I think my weight will make to a fifty foot boat.

'No difference at all,' I tell him. 'But just watch me break their morale.' Sure enough we soon see legs dangling over the side on the other boat; I am ready when it is time to tack and leap into action. We are through the wind while the other crew is still climbing back on deck and leave them standing.

The charter follows for about ten minutes but we are

leaving him far behind; he turns about heading back to where we had first met him. Meanwhile we have a good belly-laugh about our brief encounter with the Yanks.

I think it is going to end up being a dull day right up until we call at the bar for happy hour. Trev tells me that I should go to a nearby hotel for a night out with the Yanks who are holding a party. It doesn't appeal to me so I go to the "Ifo, Ifo" instead. Eseta isn't there; it turns out she's gone to the hotel as she expected me to be there. She comes in later with her sister Kato and I arrange to meet her tomorrow. Kato says I should expect Eseta to want to stay with me in England for good and I think that is a fine idea.

I am awake early this morning full of beans; my ulcers are better and I am to sort things with Eseta. Trev drops me off at the bar; when Eseta arrives in a taxi we drive to immigration where we are given a few hints to help us with our trip. One woman says to me,

'You must be Eseta Moses' boy friend.'

I ask how she knows of me and she replies that everyone knows.

'Here man, how old are you?' she then asks.

'I'm over twenty one,' I reply and she laughs and tells me, 'You are a very lucky boy.'

I go to the bar later to find her just going with her friends for a leaving party; I stay in the bar and when I'm ready to leave I get a lift back to the boat with a local man.

Ady has left overnight on a tour of the islands; Trev is in a foul mood when I come to so I go for a saunter around town only this time at my own pace. I call in the bar for a full breakfast; Eseta has left a note saying she will meet me at 1400 hours. There is plenty to be done when I return to the boat; my first job is to clean out the anchor locker. We have a tin of anti-fouling paint in it but the tin has a slight leak and is messing things up; what I don't know is that the lid was replaced by Trev and is damaged. When I lift the tin out paint is blown everywhere; I have to spend a long time cleaning up the splashes.

I meet Eseta at 1400 hours and she takes me around town

shopping. It is far easier with her as it helps to have someone who speaks the local language; she also knows the cheapest shops and ensures that I am not ripped off. Later I take her and a friend to have a look round the boat. She is very impressed but I forget to get the girls to take off their shoes and Trev turns grumpy; he is never to let it drop for days. His problem really is that he has spent all morning sewing the damaged Genoa but when he reached the foot it was torn the full width of the sail; he has had to take it for a sail-maker to fix.

I am sitting in the Mermaid Bar minding my own business this evening when I am joined by a woman for a chat. It turns out she's heard my accent and it has drawn her interest. She is married to a Yankee but originates from Morley, my home town. We are still in conversation when I hear another woman who I have never seen before asking around for someone to point me out to her. I am totally amazed when she comes straight to me and after lifting her skirts squats on my lap. My previous conversation with her friend was turning slightly amorous and I am just going through a bout of localised rigor mortis; unfortunately the woman is caught plumb centre. A look of surprise comes to her face, but not to be deterred she rides me like a National winner. Her friend sitting beside me is really shocked and shouts,

'Can't you control yourself?' 'Control myself!' The jockey says laughing with glee. 'It's the first time I've arrived since leaving Seattle.'

She rises from my lap for a moment then thinks better of it and straddles my knee, so I give her a good shake up.

It is now that her husband introduces himself; it seems he is a man of few words as he just picks me up and throws me over his shoulder. When he starts to spin I know he is angry and about to throw me, so I get him in a head lock and yell,

'If I go then so does your bloody neck.'

The man puts me down gently and at the same time apologises for his wife's behaviour; Trev orders me off the boat that night. He complains that the reason no one will talk to him is that I interfere with their wives and it is time that I went but as usual by morning he's completely forgotten.

It is now time to book out of Tonga and be on our way again. I call to see Eseta to let her know that we are all ready for off but at the last minute she tells me that she dare not sail. I go back to the Mermaid pretty upset and stay there until Eseta walks in and tells me that she is sorry about everything but she is scared of sailing. We go to a disco in town where I end up so drunk that I just go and lie down in the road on a dinghy dock and fall asleep.

I am wakened by two local fishermen who give me some of their food and take me back to *Antinea*. When I meet Eseta again the next day she tells me that she had to leave early too as she drank too much and was ill. She says again that she is very sorry about the whole thing but really is too scared to sail on the boat. I explain that this would probably be the last time we will ever see one another as Trev and me are eating out that night and will be leaving early in the morning.

At 1000 hours we are under way. It is only a short trip of half an hour before we must anchor as we are both suffering from the runs; we have noticed it usually occurs after we've eaten out. I am having other problems too; a lot of my mosquito bites are starting to fester.

We've only been on the anchorage for a couple of hours when we get a call from Ady to join him at Pop Ou Beach Resort. Once there Ady demonstrates his new world charts on a CD; the package is really impressive. We go to the Austrian's restaurant for a quiet evening but when we get there, surprise, surprise, in there is the woman who had been jogging my memory in the Mermaid but this time their party leaves early.

A good time is had by all but once again my appetite deserts me, and I don't feel too good at all.

Our plan for morning is to sail on to Hunga; we are up early to be greeted by beautiful sunshine but fate strikes once again. Trev is going through the ship's papers when he looks up with a long face. He has just seen that our visa is about to expire; I think, "What a lovely surprise, the only place we can get an extension is Neiafu and who do I know living there?"

We have a pizza at the "Ifo, Ifo" and I have a chat with my friend Eseta. There is no problem getting our visa extended so I still have time to see her again. After I give her some small presents, she says, ‘I too have something for you.’

I leave Neiafu with her address, phone number, a T-Shirt and the memory of a hug and kiss. I really believe this will be the last time I shall ever see her as I have no new ideas on how it can be otherwise. Once again we sail to Hunga for a good night at the bar.

Chapter 19

Ha'apai Group – Sailing into Stormy Waters

The next day is miserable; it has rained all through the night and is fairly cold too. Trev says we are leaving for the Ha'apai Island Group and we must get through the passé by 1000 hours, no matter what. As usual the six P's are forgotten in the rush to leave, "Proper Preparation Prevents Piss Poor Performance".

The weather and our route haven't been studied, nor has any forward planning taken place; it comes as no surprise to end up with 36 knots, of wind on the nose and sixty miles to cover. There is no possible way we will be dropping the anchor in daylight.

After sailing twenty-five miles in atrocious conditions Trev asks me if I think we should go back. I answer him.

'No, we are here so let's stick at it.'

My reasoning is that if we go back there is no way we can risk the passé into Hunga or anywhere else for that matter. The seas get so bad that one very large wave takes the screen out of the spray dodger; from then on we are absolutely saturated. By 1900 hours we are at our way-point and the high power lamp won't work.

'It's always given trouble,' Trev says. 'Just shake the fittings.'

When it does light we see that if we want to be in a depth where we can drop the anchor, then we will be on a lee shore right under the cliffs; there is only one safe thing to do and that is to go on. The chart shows a small crescent-shaped island not many miles away that offers some sort of protection from the storm, or at least it appears so. As the night is pitch black we have to be totally reliant on our plot and the GPS but from past experience of the way we have negotiated a passé using instruments only. I know that if our chart is correct then we will be all right.

The island is surrounded by a reef with the area we need L-shaped and awkward to navigate in to; we edge slowly to our way-point and drop the anchor. Wind still screams overhead but at least we have some respite from the high seas; we know we must be close to our intended position but make a unanimous decision not to indulge in sundowners. As we are soaked and absolutely knackered, we take a hot shower and go off to bed for a sound sleep.

The next morning is bright with the wind down to 25 knots. I am delighted to find that we are anchored exactly as planned; still bouncing about, but what the hell? After a pot of coffee each we are on our way again back into the big seas. In no time at all the wind is back up to 35 knots on the nose but we are rested and can see where we are going. Ha'ano, the nearest safe anchorage, is over twelve miles away; we pass through one squall after another before getting there. We choose an anchorage behind the reef; though it is tricky to get to it offers excellent protection from the storm as we can get close to the land.

Every thing goes according to plan and we are soon safely anchored. We again take hot showers followed by hot coffee laced with Chivas Regal; it is like taking knockout drops and we are asleep in minutes. I sleep soundly for three hours after which I feel much better. The wind is still screaming but at least the sun has come out, and we aren't getting thrown all over the place. I notice for the first time that we are not alone; another yacht has anchored only about fifty yards away. A quick call on the VHF and we are invited to join them later. Chris and Tom are a very nice New Zealand couple. We have drinks and snacks during which time we all agree that it will be best to stay here until the wind drops; we all unwind as we chat.

I go to my bed by 1030 hours and have a really good night's kip but first I have to dress the ulcers that have appeared on my legs. There are nine the size of carbuncles and they are just as painful.

The weather is beautiful when I wake at 0730 hours, hot sun, flat sea and no wind; absolute heaven. We begin work on the damaged spray hood then take the dinghy ashore. There is a track that leads the length of the island; we walk through two villages and for the first time I see that they both have perimeter fences. This is because they have domesticated their animals; usually pigs and hens etc. just run wild and are killed for food by anyone who takes a fancy. There are also nursery farms growing experimental crops to try and improve the diet. A local woman and her little daughter join us; she tells us quite a lot about the island. There are three villages in all linked by this one road; all children are compelled by law to go to school from five years of age until they reach twelve. After the age of twelve, education is self funded resulting in many parents being unable to educate their children further. Electricity is being brought to the island but she doubts that anyone will be able to afford to use it.

When we arrive back on the seashore the tide has left the dinghy high and dry and we have to carry it a long way out across the reef. An early night and a long sleep is the order of the day; I think it is a case of catching up after a hectic three or four weeks in Vavau. I check my legs when I wake up next day. Some sores have healed but most are so swollen that I have to lance them to let out the pus.

I need to check out the earth-grounding circuit and find that the strap was so rotten someone has removed and slung part of it; but no problem; I rewire the whole lot. When it's done the anchor is raised and we are under way to Foa about five miles away.

The passé on the chart looks a nightmare but in reality it isn't too bad. This island of Foa is surprisingly tidy and the people are friendly. We trek along a track through the bush until we reach an oasis; actually The Oasis Beach Club where we have a couple of cold beers before heading back to the boat. Once on board and in the cockpit we let our hair down for a change and get totally sozzled.

Trev comes up with a good idea; we fit a piece of timber to protect the toe rail close to the rear winch and this helps in a big way when we are raising the stern anchor.

Our next port of call, Pangai, is on the island of Lifuka ten miles away; to get there really puts our navigation to the test but as always we get in without problems. We get a pleasant surprise on arriving, a new harbour has been built that is not shown on our chart and so for the first time in months we can anchor in flat calm water. The town is a nice tidy place with a lot of new projects being built, funded by Australia. We find a little bar and visit it that evening and eat a Chinese meal and drink seven beers all for a grand total of £8 each.

I get talking to a girl from Neiafu, who goes to the "Ifo, Ifo" and knows Eseta. She tells me to write out a post card and hand it to her for when she next goes home. My sores are now really on the mend but the next day we both have another bout of the runs; of course we have eaten out again. It is a Sunday and a good day to relax which we do while listening to the local choirs belting out hymns in the church. Having heard nothing from *Da Capo* for a week we have no idea where they are and neither have cause for concern.

While enjoying another good evening in the bar we discuss our next port of call, Uoleva, six miles away. The sea is calm and there is only a light breeze and yet we manage to make the short journey by sail alone. On the way there we sight a humpback whale and calf and as always it is an outstanding sight.

A Swedish couple joins us almost as soon as we drop our hook. They issue an invitation to meet them on the beach for a barbecue that night; we accept of course and are later joined by a New Zealand couple. After the meal I lie on the beach and am quickly followed by the girl from New Zealand. We have a pleasant chat while the rest of the party sit about around the fire. There are many couples sailing the world very similar to this couple, unmarried but staying together for years until someone else comes along; they may part company or go on to have a brief affair without any complaint from their partner; tonight this girl is in such a situation but in the wrong place. We talk of our lives but I make it clear it is the wrong time for her to be jumping ship; she is still very affectionate, besotted even to the point that she is more than willing to leave her shipmate come bed mate without the slightest concern for him. It has seemingly been a successful event for all except Trev and her.

He starts on again as soon as we are back aboard; according to him it is my fault nobody talked to him although it seems odd that everyone spoke to me. Although I have different topics to talk about other than the one of being a very successful butcher, and how much money he paid for his yacht. I am beginning to think it is time to call it a day as I am hearing this too regularly lately. I have a long think about my future before I fall asleep that night and one option is to return to Neiafu and see what happens and then take it from there. We need to check for water entering the bilge and find a definite crack adjacent to one of the keel bolts. The same day we make contact with Ady through a relay boat; and shortly after direct contact is made with him. He is to join us at Lofangra, an island not very far away. The anchorage we go to is very exposed but we've been in worse before and are quite happy to stay there for a while.

As soon as we go ashore we are met by a local man, Daniel, who insists on us visiting his little farm. It is only a patch cleared on the bush but I can see that he is very proud of it and tell him what a wonderful project it is. He gives us a bag full of paw paw and tells us to call on him again tomorrow.

Back on *Antinea* we think it will be a good idea to scout out and try to find a more sheltered anchorage in the lee of the island. Off we go in the dinghy and find a lovely little place that is cut off from the large waves by a raised shelf and when we are finally anchored we find it ideal. Ady gets in touch again asking us to stay put until he meets up with us.

We pay another visit to Daniel the next day as he asked us to and find him working with several friends; it comes as a shock when we suddenly find ourselves surrounded by men wielding large knives. We needn't have worried though as they have only come to cut us a stack of bananas, pineapples, and a further selection of fruit and veg. There is enough to fill a wheelbarrow when they are finished and Daniel has a youth wheel it to the shore for us. He also adds a giant water melon to the pile as it is wheeled across the island. We delight him by giving him a bottle of rum and some tins of food.

Ady meets up with us during the afternoon; it is time for another re-union party before leaving Lofangra late the next morning en route for the island of Haa-Feva ten miles away.

Ady has seen the state of the ulcers on my legs and he gives me a six-day course of antibiotics that work wonders; in a few days all my sores are a thing of the past. We have a few drinks on *Antinea* with Ady and catch up on what we've all been up to. Trev and I pay a visit to the island that results in the usual scenario. We take a short walk around the village then it's,

'Let's get back to the boat, there's not much here.'

I would like to stay to talk to the locals and learn of their ways; maybe what we would learn could even come in handy in the future, but lately it seems we never have the time. What a waste of golden opportunities.

We hold a party on *Da Capo* for Trev's sixty-third birthday; we have rum, coke, and plenty of wine to swill down Ady's famous vodka jellies. Lucy makes a superb meal and we all have an absolutely brilliant time.

I expect that we will be sticking together for quite a while due to the water leak on *Antinea* that now stands at eighteen gallons a day seeping in.

I am awakened at 0900 hours the next morning and am just in time to watch the ferry leaving the island; I reflect that the ferry could be a good way of touring the islands if ever I decide to come back on my own.

Ady and Lucy met a beautiful young Tongan woman yesterday and got invited to her home for a meal. When they came back they told me she is a twenty-seven year old who lives with her five year old brother and a husband she detests as he won't work and beats her regularly. That seems to be the usual pastime with Tongan men and one that I don't like to see. The first time I see the girl she is pushing a barrow full of coconuts from out of the forest to a pig pen about half a mile away.

When we are all together again on the boat we discover a big problem. Ady and I get close to the keel bolts while Trev dives under the boat and kicks the keel; we can't fail to see definite movement at most of the cracks and that prompts us not to attempt the 1200-mile trip to New Zealand until a repair has been carried out. There is a marina in Fiji that owns a boat lift big enough to cope with *Antinea* and as *Da Capo* is going to accompany us as a safety boat we decide we are prepared to risk the 500-mile trip there instead. There is also the chance that I can sort something out for Eseta too as the prospect seems far better than it would be from New Zealand.

Once again the problem leak has arisen due to Trev jumping in without looking when he first bought the boat. He saved himself money by not getting a proper survey carried out. Instead of getting an independent surveyor he settled for one used by the charter firm that sold him the boat. It would have cost far less than the two bloody thousand quid spent on wine and saved him a lot more money into the bargain.

Chapter 20

Fiji, No Wine but Plenty of Ice Lollies

On the 18th October we are up early and away by 0930 hours heading for Lautoka on the island of Viti Levu, Fiji. The Genoa is poled out and we are sailing gull-winged at 8 knots; we are experiencing lovely weather and it is a pleasure to be sailing. Unfortunately our stocks of fresh food are about done. We've no bread, meat, or milk, but we do have plenty of wine. I am not too sure about how much fuel we have. I like to brim the tanks at every opportunity as it's the only way you can feel confident.

Trev has calculated that we should be arriving on the Sunday but it is better to wait and not speculate. By 1830 hours things are changing, the wind has increased to 27 knots and we have to gybe although we still keep our speed. The temperature begins to fall so fast that I have to wear my fleece to keep warm; I am starting to feel homesick too but thinking things out when on watch helps and of course the time seems to pass quicker. Even though it is a bitterly cold night I enjoy myself; the moon is out and I am delighted to be doing some real sailing again.

We have a dull start to the next day but by1000 hours the sun comes out and we hoist the spinnaker. It's an absolute bastard to do as our dinghy lies on the foredeck and is always right in the way. Even when we get the kite up I'd swear we go no faster and it only stays up half an hour making matters worse when it gets wrapped around the forestay on the way down.

The wind gets up at dusk and even with both sails reefed we maintain a constant speed of 10.5 knots throughout the night. I have another pleasant time on watch followed by a couple of hours sound sleep but when I awake Trev tells me that the alternator isn't charging again. I try to repair it but it is completely burnt out and will have to be replaced. Trev gets out a new unit he bought in England; it is a completely different type and will have to be modified. The only option is to get the generator set out but then we have another problem: there is no fuel for it. In desperation I get out some two-stroke mixture that was intended for the outboard engine and in a shit or bust attempt the thing starts up immediately.

At 1400 hours and doing 6 knots we pass through the outer islands of Tonga, heading west. Ady catches a large mari mari, a dolphin fish, so at the first opportunity we sail alongside and get a share of it; as we draw near they throw the fish and I make a great save. It is cooked and eaten at once and while I wash the dishes after our meal Trev goes out on deck and lands another 25lb dolphin fish; we'll be eating well again tomorrow. The boat is still going so well it seems we should be at Fiji by Monday evening.

It is at this point that I decide to let fate take over my life instead of holding back from everyone and believe me, once in Fiji I really go on the rampage.

I stand watch until 1400 hours compensated by a sound sleep until 0630 hours. On waking up I find that we are in sight of Viti Levu, the main island, and our destination. The boat is doing a steady 9 knots and we are having a lovely sail. I see that we are leaving a large freighter to starboard that is standing unusually high in the water, about seven miles from land; the odd thing is that it doesn't appear to be moving and eventually we realise it is perched on a reef. This is yet another reminder that one must stay alert at all times in these waters. We find once again on reaching our way-point that it is well short of where Trev has estimated; there are still a further forty-five miles to sail, we won't be reaching port tonight after all. After we've negotiated a dog leg passé through the barrier reef we drop anchor in a large bay for the night with the satisfaction of knowing that we will certainly be in the marina tomorrow.

Quite a selection of food has passed our lips today, fish, fish, and now yet more fish followed by several gin and tonics; it is time to catch up on some shut-eye. Trev wakes me up about 0545 hours but I find out from Ady that local time is only 0430 hours, what next? After eating a light breakfast our voyage is finished by motor sailing into Lautoka. The sea state in the anchorage is almost gale conditions when we leave *Antinea* to visit customs and immigration. We are grateful to get ashore and leave the dinghy bouncing like a cork beside the jetty.

Paper work in Fiji is an absolute nightmare; many of the lengthy forms have to be completed in triplicate and done separately as there is no carbon paper. The task is made worse by Yankee crews' constant whingeing; they just won't get on with the job in hand. I can see the funny side of it all as the officials are not in the least put out by all the grumbling; to them it is probably most entertaining.

I thought we would have a big problem at customs as we have to make a declaration of excess liquor on board. I've learned in the past not to give out information unless it's asked for and to always tell the truth, yet Trev contradicted these beliefs. We had hidden several dozen bottles under the cockpit leaving the rest for bonding in a cabin for when the customs officer came on board. Trev makes it clear that we do indeed exceed our quota of liquor but gives a low estimate of the true amount and also offers the guy some wine and spirits as a gift. In my book that can easily be interpreted as bribery. It is plain to see that the customs officer is uneasy but he is kind and diplomatic about it saying,

'No, thank you, I don't drink much.'

He does, however, with a little persuasion accept a $12 tip. While sealing the cabin he asks if we would like a few bottles leaving out to consume during our stay. I would have answered yes, but Trev says,

'We've done that already.' And knowing we have a lot more, signs a declaration that the amount mentioned earlier is the total on board; if they had carried out a search we would be right in the shit. I myself am glad that I was not asked for a signature as a refusal might have offended.

When we came here I was led to believe that the repairs were to be done through the insurance company and properly supervised by a surveyor, but now he is talking about finding some cheap local labour. At one point he even suggests that we dry and clean the keel to hull area and pack the gap with sealant. I argue that it just isn't good enough and Ady too tells him it is a waste of time.

In the end he concedes and agrees to contact his brother-in-law, who is an insurance investigator, to seek advice. Consequentially a surveyor comes to the marina to examine the boat, which by then has been lifted from the water. A marine engineer is employed at the same time to carry out any repairs needed; the whole deal appears on the surface to be okay. However in a short time things take a turn for the worse; in my opinion the surveyor and the workers are not as good at their jobs as they have made out they are.

Antinea is lowered into a hurricane hole, a slot in the ground similar to a pit used in car maintenance. The keel fits into the pit while the hull lies close to the ground supported by old tyres thus offering a smaller area to strong winds. We already suspect the damage is bad before we drop the keel but find it far worse than anyone has envisaged. It is thought to have taken a violent shock at sometime (I can remember two of them) as one keel mounting bolt has sheered and the hull around every bolt hole has been shattered; a trip straight to New Zealand could well have proved fatal for us.

We pass most of our time in town or at the Yacht Club; every thing is even cheaper here than in Tonga. Beer is 60p a bottle of 4.6% proof and meals average about £3 each. I manage to contact England and talk to Tracey. I tell her about Eseta and ask her, without success, to contact immigration for me. I get the message.

The marina is thrown into total confusion after we plug into shore power and turn the air conditioner on. I check the spec. plate details to find the unit only works on 110v; the shore power is 240v, should I really be surprised?

We spend another night in the club and have a pleasant chat with some girls working on the site but we are still up and about very early the next day. Trev suggests having our evening meal at the nearby Resort Club and this time it is me who thinks the food is crap. It costs us $60 each, a complete waste of money; but of course the meal does have a have a fancy French name.

My e-mail address has been cancelled and I am told that someone else is now using it; I was so confident that no one else could think of the same one that I contact the service provider; it is immediately reinstated. I send an e-mail to Eseta telling her I've found a way to get her to England and I shall return for her and she will be in England for Christmas.

Around the marina are about four shower blocks as well as a large main one. The small ones are in units of four showers and only supply cold water but they are superb. I could call in for several showers each day simply to cool down. There is no need to take a towel, just put shorts back on after the shower and you are dry in minutes. After taking an early dowse I feel great with a good appetite for breakfast.

I take a look at the repairs and see that the way they are going we could be here for quite a long time; the guy running the workshop has given Trev a rough estimate of around two to three thousand US dollars but the hourly rate is only $15 Fijian, about five pounds. I can see by the speed at which the men are working it could work out to be a very expensive job as sometimes there are as many as four at a time on the job and often only two working while the others watch on. I also notice that they gradually start later of a morning and finish earlier; I think I am doing the right thing to keep a record of their actual hours.

We have a rewarding trip to town; it is about eleven kilometres at a cost of $10 each way by taxi. We take a stroll around the large market and send off several e-mails. I also meet a French couple who have sailed on the Catamaran *Magic Cat* and know Marina; they too are very sad that she is no longer sailing with us.

Of late I have taken up hard exercise, over sixty sit-ups and press-ups every day; my stomach muscles are hardening up and I am becoming really fit. Every afternoon I take lunch at the marina café at $6 a time. It is a proper bargain. As the days pass by I am to spend a lot of time there and make friends with the girls who run the place. We go to the yacht club at night too and although we are having a good time we eventually realise that the young guy who works here is ripping us off and decide to put a stop to him.

We have another trip to town and on the way ask the taxi driver where we can find some proper girls who will take all and say nowt. We are fixed up at once for the same night with two lovely Indian lasses who know their stuff; I am on top form and rise to the occasion. At thirteen quid a throw I have to make a pig of myself; I even have a second helping.

After lunch next day, the lasses in the cafe keep giving me funny looks and on the way back to the boat several people shout to me,

'Don't be late tonight.' There is only one person who knew so I go to the taxi stand and give our driver a proper Scarborough Warning.

I really amaze myself that night. I don't usually have much of an appetite but now I am drinking like a fish and eating like an ox so I decide that from then on instead of getting a Chinese takeaway I will go for an Indian instead.

Trev doesn't believe me when I tell him that everyone knows of our night out, but that is until we pass through the security gate after leaving the Yacht Club. A security guard who we haven't seen before asks if tonight's girls were as good as the ones the night before; that really leaves Trev pulling a face.

I am kept busy this morning repairing the fibreglass diving platform and then it's over to the café where I spend a couple of hours chatting with the lasses over a few beers. I see several yachts leaving for New Zealand during the afternoon.

Tonight we are going to square things with the prat behind the bar in the Yacht Club. We sit where all the customers are in earshot and coax him into admitting that he may have made a big mistake but persuade him he will make it right, one way or the other. We get through quite a few beers and even treat him to one or two; I can still hear him shouting when we get up to walk out and leave him to square the bill himself. We don't see him again for several days and when he is at work again we never hear a single mention of our ploy; from then on he is honest, leastways with us he is.

There are several Fijians building a large supply boat. It looks similar to a landing craft and is to be used as a mobile shop visiting the various islands. When the sun gets high at midday they usually come and sit with me in the shade of *Antinea* and have a chat. They are only paid £1 an hour in wages and although the work is very hard they need to put in sixteen hours a day just to make a living. I have a very high regard for all of them as they are a really nice, honest, hardworking bunch. Amongst them is a woman welder, who hardly ever stops working.

When out shopping one day we found a shop that was selling twenty-four pint cans of beer for Fijian $29. Today we ask the usual taxi driver to take us the same shop to pick up a few cases but he takes us to a friend of his instead. The driver must have pre-warned his friend on the radio as there are already six cases waiting for us on the counter. When we ask the shop owner how much they are he answers,

'Very, very cheap; only Fijian $34 each.'

We tell him he can put them all back in stock and tell our driver,

'From now on you'll go where you're asked and don't even think about creaming commission from our purchases or spouting your mouth off.'

The hull repair is still going at a snail's pace yet Trev continues to insist that we will be away in about a week; I know different as they haven't even begun making the usual lame excuses.

The taxi driver is to finally score a few points back from us. Elephantiasis is an epidemic in Fiji and everyone is invited to collect a free dose of pills to prevent it. He arranges off his own back for us to go to a police station to take our doses and we are truly grateful.

One evening in the Yacht Club we meet the welder woman and a workmate, George; we finish up at a disco in town. I can't for the life in me remember what I said to the welder but whatever it was it certainly appealed to her maternal instincts.

I don't wake up until 1130 hours the morning after but I am soon okay; Trev tells me that I am only safely on the boat because a guard carried me up the ladder to the cockpit and that when we got to the dinghy the tide was out. There was no way I was capable of climbing down the wall so he called the guard to help him. They tried to lower me steadily but instead let me slip and luckily I fell into the dinghy.

Instead of a breakfast at the café I try the hair of the dog and I am surprised to be joined by George and the lady welder. I buy them a beer each and spend the rest of the afternoon with the welder's hand up my trouser leg. When they finally leave I feel as though I've been made redundant; I believe that's what it is called when you've just had the golden handshake

There is a celebration going off amongst the workers on the big boat when I wake up next morning. The boat owner and his wife are celebrating a Hindu holiday. Everyone is treated to iced fruit juice and fancy cakes and I am invited the moment I stick my head through the hatch.

I receive an e-mail from Eseta saying that she wants to be my Friendly Island girl. She's become aware of what a lucky girl she is and realises that I was telling the truth when I told her she would be in England with me before Christmas.

I am prepared for another lazy day while Trev is away trying to speed up the boat repairs and to get the insurance surveyor to re-examine the boat. I go out to sit with the workers but today only the welder is there; I invite her for a beer and a look around the boat. She has been here about an hour when suddenly she says,

'Arthur, please let me sit on you.'

What else can I say except 'Okay then, if you must.'

It takes at least five minutes to drag the boiler suit over her steel toe-capped boots and then I am taken over the moon at breakneck speed. She asks if it will be all right for her to call for more every day and we shake hands on it. I am just about to climb back down the ladder when she turns on me and asks if I will give her some money.

'Money? What do you know about money?' I try telling her she should learn to ask for it first but when she tells me what it will be used for, I am really touched and give her some. She says – and with a straight face too. "Please, Arthur, I am so hot I would like to buy an ice lollipop." I can afford to keep a dozen more like her.

She must have been talking out of turn in the café because from then on it costs me a small fortune in ice lollipops.

Summer has arrived, the weather becomes red hot and I am

spending so much time at the café that it is fast becoming my second home; it is really cool in there.

Ady has been away for a day or two and comes back to see how work on *Antinea* is progressing as he wants to be on his way to New Zealand. I am in the Yacht Club with him one day when we hear someone shouting,

'Help me, Arthur.'

I look out but see no one until Ady points and says,

'Over there, look, it's a girl in the water that's calling.'

It is one of the girls from the cafe swimming in the passé: I jump down to meet her as she climbs from the water and ask what is wrong.

'Nothing,' she replies. 'Not now.'

As soon as we are in the long grass I take a look in a bag she is carrying. It holds about a dozen limpets and a sea slug; she tells me they are for lunch, ugh! I persuade her to leave them and have an ice lollipop instead then I treat her to a proper lunch.

Ady and Lucy join us at the Yacht Club later but it is only to tell us they will be on their way the following day; I call Tonga and tell Eseta to start packing as Trev is about to blow his top with the workers. I've taken a look at the repairs and mention that it could be done better but I am told to keep my nose out as they are doing their best. One of the things that we did in my business was to repair forty-foot fibreglass trailers so I know what I'm talking about and it makes me angry to see him being ripped off.

I chat with a young Indian girl who virtually runs the marina; she asks if I would like to take her back to England as a companion. I tell her that I certainly would but she lives just one island too far and I am already fully booked.

I have to start using a net as the mosquito's they are becoming a damn nuisance at night. Trev has bought a 110 volt transformer and I soon have the air conditioner working until a pipe to the mains water tap bursts. I get a new vinyl coupler and some special sealant which has to be left to harden for half an hour before use. I've only just repaired it when I see Trev shaking the repair nest. A workman then had a go, but between them they gave the glue no chance to harden and when we turn the water on and it leaks I leave them to it with a new joint and sealer while I go to cool off in the café.

I am called back to the boat; some stainless steel plates have been fabricated to fit over the keel bolts and spread the load but the bolt holes were drilled slightly off centre and the plates won't fit. The intention is to get them altered after the weekend; what can I do about it? I tell the man in charge of the operation to get me a round file and to bugger off from the job until morning when they will be ready. It takes me hours to file the holes out and my arms ache badly when the job is done but the plates fit like a glove; there is no excuse for them but to now get stuck in and get the job finished. Even then it's well over another week before they are ready to refit the keel.

When they eventually drop the hull onto the keel it takes them from 0700 to 1900 hours; I stay out of the way while they are doing this because when I make any suggestions I am interfering and so I think "bollocks" to it.

We are getting closer to leaving and all sorts of situations begin to crop up. For one thing the lad running the bar brings in two nice girls; he tries to get me to take one of them, along with him and the other one, to club land. I ask him how much cash they all have between them When it turns out to be not very much I tell him to keep them on a low heat and I may be back next year. Even the older women are becoming frisky; I get no end of invitations to their homes for a meal. There is one woman, a worker in the Yacht Club, she wears horn-rimmed spectacles and Trev has named her Mugabe. She invites me to breakfast and all sorts of things, until one night when she closes the bar after holding my hand most of the evening I ask her where she is going next.

'Home to bed,' she replies.

I tell her I will go with her and lay on something warm but she replies.

'I'm so sorry, but I'm very tired.'

I ask her if I can take that as a definite maybe.

The next morning she comes to say she hasn't been able to sleep all night for thinking about me. When she comes round again I tell her that I'll chat her friend up instead as I think she will be too knackered after lying awake all night.

We spend a busy morning putting anti-foul paint on the hull and while Trev has a sleep I go to the café to cool down. Two of my favourite girls ask,

'What is your most preferred food in England?' I tell them, 'Fish and chips wrapped in newspaper.'

I see a knowing wink pass between them but nothing more is said until I see them the next day. I have called in and just sit drinking cold beers; about half an hour before they normally close they come and sit at my table. We are having a very intimate conversation when a Yankee comes in asking for service. When the girls tell him they are shut for the day he gets a bit sharp and asks why I am still here. One lovely lass answers,

'We are waiting for him to leave.'

When he has gone I tell them I am sorry to be holding them back and that I will leave now. The girl hugs me and begins crying.

'Yes, I am staying here till you leave but please, I don't want you to go. We've made your favourite meal for a party.'

They both open their bags and pull out newspaper parcels. When they unwrap them, each parcel contains a fish head and some cold slices of sweet potato. What can I say? They look so proud and yet they are so poor; this is all they can afford. I get stuck in and eat the lot, then they both pose while I take their photos and give them a hug and a kiss; they are crying their eyes out when they leave.

Trev has been busy too. He has finally got his bill. It is US$7300 and he is furious. It turns out that while I was secretly taking note of the hours worked he was doing the same and our times, which are very similar, bear no resemblance to those on the bill. Trev, none too kindly, points this out and achieves a substantial reduction.

A new day sees me up the mast fixing the windex and fitting a fender on the top shroud spreader. Trev has arranged for a young girl to come to give the boat a really good clean, having already worked out a price for the job. When she arrives she is accompanied by her mother and cousin; the cousin is a lad who sometimes works behind the Yacht Club bar.

We leave them to it and go off into Lautoka to check out at immigration. Par for the course is that Trev has lost the main document we need but the lady in the office is kind and still lets us through. We do a spell of shopping purchasing groceries and beer, finally calling at customs to have the seals removed from our liquor store. I think we are both surprised when we are told that we can remove them ourselves with the instruction,

'But you must not drink anything until you are out in the open sea.'

When we arrive back at the boat the cleaners have done a lovely job but when Trev pays them they all scuttle off without a word. The way that they skedaddle we think that they must have all been expecting a full wage each.

This time before we leave the fuel tanks are filled to the brim and some spare cans too; we take on fresh water and prepare for the rising tide when we can clear through the passé. I have a few bob left in Fijian currency so pay my last visit to the café and share it amongst the girls who have worked so hard to make my stay here a time to remember. I enjoy a good time and most of them have given me one.

Chapter 21

New Zealand Here I Come

We are away at 1500 hours and as we clear the passé and look back, all the girls are sitting on the rocks waving farewell. The forecast is for stormy weather but our idea is that we are sure to get bad times on the way so we may as well have it at the beginning of the voyage while we are still fresh.

It is 1500 hours 12th November when we leave. A big tropical storm is coming up behind us but we go on undeterred. Winds of 33 knots hit us and soon we are literally flying at 9 knots; the seas are up and we suffer a lot of water hitting us in the cockpit but it is great to be sailing again. I have a sleep until going on watch at 2400 hours when I manage to keep the speed at 7 knots but have to steer a little off course to achieve it. I sleep through to 0715 hours. After I come off watch at 1415 hours it is a lovely surprise to find that the day starts much better than the one I left last night and the sea is much more settled. We are able to shake out all reefs from the sails and while having a fantastic sail I get to thinking again about my plans for after we reach New Zealand.

I feel sure that I am doing the right thing; there will be many places to go and things to do when we reach England and I may be able to forget the pain I've had in recent times and hopefully start anew. We contact Ady; he has been having a hard time and now he is slowed by light winds and still at least another two days to go. He also tells us that the old home country is on high alert because of threats from terrorists. We sail along at 7 knots and hold our course all day. I am back on watch at 0230 hours under a clear half moon that makes vision good but it sure is getting colder. We've done 230 miles by now with 830 remaining.

When the moon goes down we are still doing 6 knots and the sea is flat and once again I am off on my day dreaming. I am out in the cold and darkness, so what the hell am I doing here when I could be home in bed, warm but alone? That last word always snaps me out of it and I give myself a talking to, reminding myself that I am taking part in a great adventure that I would never have wanted to miss. Day break brings another wild time on the Pacific. The seas get up very high and I am soaked all the time but who the hell cares? This is the life. I go to bed 0630 to 0830 hours and enjoy a really deep sleep; within minutes of getting up I have a bad fall as I am washing the dishes. The boat falls off a wave and I am thrown straight across the cabin and onto my back, I manage to protect my head but give one of my elbows a nasty whack. Ady phones at 1100 hours; he too has taken a bad fall and now his arse is black and blue.

We've been romping on for some time now and maybe we can be there in four days. By 1400 hours the seas have eased and we are much warmer and yet still retain 23 knots of wind. I stand my watch from 0030 to 0600 hours. Still feeling wide awake I let Trev have the benefit. It is a good night and I maintain 7 knots throughout with the wind just forward of the port beam. The only problem I have is that the Global Positioning System display keeps going off but I put a plot on the chart whenever it returns until it eventually rights itself.

I am ready for a sleep when I come off duty and get my head down until 1030 hours then I wake up to a beautiful day and find our speed up to 9 knots. Ady calls again and tells us that we should soon be passing through a large high pressure area and may be slowing down; we must be nearing it as we are already feeling much warmer.

Throughout the day I have some quite long kips and after waking from one I see Trev about to dismantle the front of the engine to fit a new impellor to the sea water pump. It would have been a complete disaster as the pump is actually situated at the back of the engine and is in quite an accessible position.

Excitement is rising now when I think about returning to England with Eseta and meeting my family. I am really hoping that they can all be friends. Trev and I are getting on like a house on fire but I do miss having a woman around. We are having a really warm day so I take my first shower since leaving Fiji and feel terrific after it. I then tackle the salt water pump myself. It is an easy task to fit the new impellor bit but I have quite a bit of difficulty getting water circulating through. However soon after priming all the system we are in working order again, which is a good thing as we are soon to lose the wind just as Ady had predicted. We have a 1.5 knot tide against us too reducing our speed over the ground to 4.5 knots but we are still enjoying it all.

Our day is spent boozing, sun bathing and trying to hold sensible conversation. At 0430 hours I go on watch to find that the wind has gone back to a westerly, which is just what we want; there are only another 330 miles to go but by 0800 hours the weather changes dramatically. A massive storm is approaching just giving us enough time to reef down both sails before hitting us with 37 knots of wind. Another reef is required in the main and both of us end up saturated.

This shit weather stays with us until 1330 hours before it eases slightly. During the storm we were pushed east but are now able to get back on course. Ady calls to let us know that he has arrived; this is excellent news. He also advises us that we can get in after dark quite easily if the call is needed and this is the sort of news a sailor likes to hear.

During the night Trev shouts me out, we have 40 knots of wind and need to reef down again but we are getting to be expert at this job. We accomplish the task with ease and after we've done Trev gets his head down for the night.

I have a good book and am about to sit back enjoying my watch when suddenly there is a violent a crash from the foredeck; I crane my neck to listen.

Yes, there is certainly something seriously wrong at the sharp end; I go down into the cabin. Thud… Thud… there is no mistaking the sound I am hearing. It has just got to be the anchor adrift from its mounting and by the sound of it; it is swinging over the side trying to smash a hole through the hull every time the boat nose dives. Before doing anything drastic I need to take a look and assess the problem. While raising the forward hatch I get swamped as the bow dives into the waves. I have to think about that one …

'Yes, got it.'

The bow is lifting as we climb another wave. It is time to

open the hatch and pull myself up confirming that it is exactly as I feared: the anchor is swinging free. As I climb back down a wave breaks over us from behind, slamming the hatch lid shut... Unfortunately my right hand is between the lid and the deck and I end up getting my forefinger crushed with a gash over the knuckle, revealing bone. I wake up Trev and apply a quick dressing while preparing to go out onto the fore deck.

'Hell, what next? It'll be almost suicide up there. It'll be certain suicide if I don't. Oh hell! Here I go.'

I clip my harness onto a jack-stay that runs from the cockpit to the foredeck and begin the slow crawl forward while Trev takes control of the helm. If I am to be washed overboard at least I'll be still attached, although climbing back on deck will be no easy task. I have just made it to the halfway mark when *Antinea* dives into an oncoming wave barely leaving me time to encompass the mast with my arms. I hang on for grim death as a wall of water strikes knocking the breath from my lungs but determination gives me the strength to hold on until the bow rises again. Releasing my hold I scramble forward making a lunge for the pulpit but don't quite make it and have to settle for grasping a teak deck rail instead. My arms are almost torn from their sockets when the next wave comes but with my adrenaline running high I manage to hold on.

This time I make the pulpit, interlacing it with arms and legs so I am braced for the next dive but I am not prepared for what follows. The boat takes me almost two metres below the surface and I have to cling on for dear life as the icy force almost drags me free, assisted by the buoyancy aids in my jacket. When we rise again there is barely a minute to grab the anchor chain and haul in what I can before being slammed into the trough, jarring every bone in my body. When the next wave hits I am laid at full stretch yet I must retain my hold on the chain. I am still there when the bow comes up, although this time the heavy anchor has to be lifted on deck. The next slam gives me a helping hand by bouncing the device high enough to be pulled over the toe rail but once again I am on a downward plunge. I have to suffer three more dippings before the anchor is lashed securely in its mountings and we are back to normal. Trev returns to his bunk while I make good the dressing on my wound and then go back to work.

At 0530 hours the wind is back up to 40 knots and a massive storm appears on the radar, heading straight for us. When it strikes we are on the point of broaching, as the auto-helm can't react quickly enough. I take us twenty degrees off course and it works a treat yet we are still getting lots of water over us. It is my worst day ever on the boat; I take a two-hour kip and as I'm sleeping Trev lands a 10lb tuna. He also makes contact with an English couple who have set out from Malta but we quickly leave them behind.

The pain from my finger is now sheer torture, even with pain killers. I down several gins and Trev lets me have a long sleep then feeling a little better I take over the watch. I re-dress the finger, which by now has stopped bleeding and I can see that it looks as bad as it feels. At this time we are motor sailing at 5.5 knots but in far better conditions and I know for certain that we will be able to put our heads down in New Zealand tonight.

We carry on under power and sail to make sure we get in early and then tie up for the night on the quarantine dock in Opua, in The Bay of Islands where the Greenpeace ship *Rainbow Warrior* was sunk. We see Ady and Lucy here but are not allowed to join them ashore.

Once again Trev comes up with his scheme to not declare all our liquor even though he knows the penalty here could be very severe. I tell him I will have no part in it as from the start he has said that he would get it all bonded.

Due to all the rope work my finger has burst open again and my hand is very swollen, so I will have to take care of it and let it rest until it has knitted together. I take pain killers and whiskey then settle down for a long night's sleep. I awake next day very stiff, probably because I have been dreaming of my trip to England. It is far cooler than I've been expecting, in fact it is just like an English April, but regardless of the temperature The Bay of Islands truly is beautiful. We pass through immigration and customs effortlessly but it is all done on trust and if it backfires I am sure they will come down hard on us. Ady takes us to Piahia and gives us a brief tour before leaving in his boat for a few days. I tell him that once I meet up with my Tongan friend Eseta, then I will let fate take its own course. He says he's going to miss me if I decide to leave but fully understands.

I contact a local travel agent to book all of the many flights I shall need and also to try and sort out an entry permit for Eseta; the travel agent's name is Meg and she is to work wonders for us.

Trev and me go to the local Yacht Club where we meet up with several old friends we've previously become acquainted with in the various places along our voyage; it is good to have a chat and find out about their experiences.

The weather turns warmer and I have a rare great appetite at breakfast, then our windlass burns out. We take it to a repair shop and pay another visit to town where I get an e-mail from the "Ifo, Ifo" saying that Eseta was getting very excited until she was teased into thinking that maybe I only want to abuse her.

After making a phone call to ask her if she really believes that, everything is soon back on line. I also find out that someone is sending regular reports about me to Tonga. During a conversation with Bryce, the owner of the "Ifo, Ifo", I mention hurting my finger and he replies,

'Yes, I know, in the anchor locker, wasn't it?'

I have never mentioned the incident before.

Trev gets his flight to England booked with his return to be on February 18th but mine is still being sorted out. Finally he also lets common sense prevail and he has the liquor put into bond. The bloke who does it even tells us to take some out to use as we require; 'so you see honesty is the best policy,' I tell Trev.

They are holding a buffet at the Marina Yacht Club. It is all right I suppose but there is no atmosphere in the place.

I watch the square rigger arriving from Tonga and later go for a chat with one of the lads off it. Summer has arrived in New Zealand and the days are getting longer; they seem even longer though by there being no news from Tonga. I visit the club and stay until the death then the next day I phone Tonga. Bryce tells me the internet has been down for a few days explaining the lack of news and that Eseta is all ready for off. I can hear her shouting. 'Yes, yes, tell him yes.'

Meg gets the fares booked and then I go to Kiri, Kiri to collect a car with Trev. He could fly down to Auckland for the same price that he pays for the car if only he wouldn't rush into things but think them out first.

We visit a Swiss restaurant and have a pleasant meal before going back to the boat for sundowners; the last few days are then spent doing repairs or relaxing.

I am in the Yacht Club when out of the blue a stranger comes across to me for a chat; he asks how it is that I can put up with Trev. He tells me that the same topic is on the lips of a lot of people he's spoken to. According to the stranger they are all saying he is a man so unsure of himself that he has to go rushing around proving to everyone how good he is, whereas they see me as entirely the opposite. I tell the stranger,

'I get on with most people simply because I agree with everyone and everything then when they have had their say I please myself anyway and do just what I want.'

I see Trev off before booking a seat on a coach to Auckland. Then I sit back to a three-day boring wait for my flight to Tonga. Trev has left me a long list of jobs to do and this helps to pass the time. Ady returns and I have a last night out in the club with him and Lucy. The next morning Ady takes me and my baggage to the bus stop.

It is a lovely trip to Auckland, a journey of 250 miles for £15, now that is peanuts. I can see the countryside in comfort and I meet an interesting old, local man on the coach who gives me information about all the sights as we drive past.

As I am alighting from the coach I can't believe my eyes when I see a woman I saw once briefly in Fiji marina though I didn't actually speak with her then. She has been travelling on the same coach and we get talking; she also is heading for the airport. Very soon she tells me to leave the organisation of getting the airport feeder bus to her. I do and she not only does this but pays my fare as well. When I tell her at the airport that we now have to go our separate ways as I am heading for Tonga she is shocked. She has assumed that like her I was flying on to England. Oh dear, another disappointed female.

Chapter 22

Collecting Eseta

The flight to Nuka Alufa passes uneventfully. Meg has arranged me a hotel for the night together with transport to and from the airport. I fly to Neiafu the following day where the taxi driver I use knows Eseta and takes me straight to her home; here I am met by her sister Ofa. She takes me to the café to wait for Eseta who is away rehearsing for a singing competition. The taxi driver tells me the fare is $40 but Ofa nearly jumps down his throat and tells him it is $10 or nothing. I have a great night out with her at the "Ifo, Ifo" bar then she takes me to stay at her brother's home for the night.

I am awakened early the next morning as some relatives have arrived out of the blue and want to stay with Eseta's brother so I am taken back to the family home. When I reach the house the girls are all still asleep and what a beautiful sight they make. They are soon up and about and I see that they are a family that is not very well off in money terms but in happiness and kindness they have a great deal of wealth. They help any waifs and strays who happen to be down on their luck and though I'm not in that category I am treated as if they have known me for years and at once I feel at home. The girls work long hours for only £10 a week, I know the cost of living here is low but not so low. A wage of only £10 a week means that they have to do without a lot of things we consider essentials. Eseta is to sing in the South Sea Island contest tonight. I have treated her to some nice clothes as she is really built up on doing well and I want her to look good. She is a natural singer, her voice a pleasure to listen to and the judges must have thought so too as she gets through to the finals. The night is a big event for the town and is held in the large community centre, the main forum of the entire island. Fetes, discos and markets are all staged in these buildings.

The next day I visit the local Beach Resort with Eseta and Ofa to celebrate. We have a nice time there then we borrow a cousin's taxi and take a case of beer out to a desolate part of the coast where we spend the rest of the afternoon relaxing and having a good chat.

We will soon have to be leaving and decide to have a party as all Tongans do; it is a barbecue behind the "Ifo Ifo" bar with all their friends and relatives. I spend a long time talking to Ofa and that's when I realise that the visit to England will not be the same unless she is there too. I've already been thinking that three months in a strange country alone with a virtual stranger could possibly prove to be a bad experience for Eseta so I ask Ofa if she will come along too. She leaps up from her seat in delight.

'Oh, Arthur, I would love to come, but are you sure?'

I wake with a thick head the next morning and though I don't regret asking Ofa to come with Eseta to New Zealand and England I reflect that if I hadn't drunk so much last night I might have given more consideration as to how much it was going to cost me; but I'm a man of my word so it's too late now.

Their mother laundered all my clothes for me yesterday, so with my packing completed we are all set for off.

Imagine my surprise at 1400 hours when a convoy of mini coaches turns up in the street packed with people I met the night before; we arrive at the airport amidst a blare of horns. This is the last part of our journey to go according to my plans. On arrival in Nuku'alofa we are taken to the hotel I have booked for the night and are to leave at 0400 hours with 13,000 miles to travel so I tell the girls that I will have an early night. I go to the nearest bank cash machine but my credit card has been blocked. This is a complete disaster as I have no other means of obtaining any money at all. Luckily it is daytime in England and I manage to catch my daughter-in-law Tracey before she leaves home to go to work. She contacts the bank for me to be told that I am the only person they can speak to sort out the problem. I have to ring the bank and after declaring my private code word I am told that I haven't exceeded my limit but have been spending larger amounts than usual. Of course they blocked my card until they were satisfied it hadn't been stolen. It is soon sorted out and I am solvent again so I take the girls to the hotel bar and have a drink with them before leaving for bed. I tell them to get anything they want and put it on my bill to sort out in the morning. This is to be my first big mistake.

I get an early call and after taking it I go to Ofa and Eseta's room. I am surprised and worried to find no one there. At reception I tell the manageress that I am concerned about them. Her response is, 'I am only worried about the rental car I got for them.'

Shocked I tell her, 'But they can't even drive.'

'Now I am *very* worried; I just thought they were drunk, they didn't say that neither of them could drive and as they were ordering a hire car I took it for granted that one of them could.'

She goes on to threaten that she will stop me leaving the island if the car isn't back.

The mini-bus is just about to leave for the airport when they come chugging down the street pulling up with a screech of brakes. What can I say? They both have big wide grins as they tell me what a good night they've had driving around.

At the airport we go to the check-in desk and I buy Ofa a ticket for New Zealand and we are just about to board when an official notices that they do not have visas and refuses to let them on the plane. I tell the official then that the information I received in Auckland was that they would be allowed in providing they stay in the departure lounge. The official still insists that it is a very definite no to them boarding.

With only minutes to spare I have to make a big decision; to stay or to go. Both Ofa and Eseta agree that I can only regain control of things if I am back in England. Regretfully I kiss them both farewell and leave.

When I arrive in Auckland three hours later I telephone them and they say,

'Not to worry, we will wait here as long as it takes for you to sort things out for us.'

The flights to Singapore and on to Manchester go without a hitch and as soon as I am back in my home at Scarborough my disappointment intensifies.

I tell my son Kevin that the Friendly Island girls are arriving soon but this news goes down like a lead balloon. Also I find that getting through to Tonga on the phone is harder than putting a man on the moon. One night I am calling from a box at the top of our street when I hear a ruckus outside the booth; when I take a look two louts outside are kicking the door. One lout shouts to me to hand over all the pound coins that I have stacked up for the calls or else they will beat me up. When I begin to show panic one of them comes to open the door; this is exactly what I am waiting for and as he reaches for the door I give it a very hard shove with my foot which has the desired effect of splitting his head open. With one down and one to go I take up the advantage and run out to face the other lout who spits right in my eyes but I still manage to kick him on his knee cap. That is lucky for him as I had aimed for his balls; but that makes two down. They pick themselves up off the floor and skedaddle sharpish.

I re-enter the phone box and phone my son Kevin who quickly drives to my home from his village a few miles away. He advises me to report the incident to the police and at the police station the officer dealing with us tells me that I have done the right thing as it will be helpful if the louts report their injuries; oddly enough I never get troubled again.

After several more attempts I finally get through to the girls who say they need cash to obtain a visa. No matter how I try I find obstacles blocking my way in my efforts to send the cash to them. Firstly, neither of the girls have a bank account.

After several frustrating attempts to get the money to them I ring Meg, the travel agent in New Zealand who arranged all my flights; she is only too pleased to send some money on to Nuka Alofa for collection from the hotel we stayed at. Meanwhile I receive an e-mail from the Ifo-Ifo saying that the girls are getting fed up of waiting and I must admit I am not surprised but then I receive another e-mail saying that they have received the money and purchased the visas and the best news is they are now on their way. I go out to my local pub and have me a private celebration.

Leaving early I drive to Manchester airport where I contact the immigration office and inform them of the unusual circumstances surrounding the girls' visit. I am advised to stay put and I will be contacted if I am needed.

The flight lands and I see the passengers leave arrivals but there is no sign of the lasses. Then suddenly there is a man beside me asking me to sit down as he wants to ask me a few questions.

"Please don't let them down now that they have got this far," I think.

He asks me, 'Who wanted you to bring them to England?' that's an easy one as I have invited them.

Next I am asked to explain why and when I tell him that for once in my life I have been given a chance to give someone an opportunity like this and I have seized it and brought them along, the immigration officer is kind and asks me how long are they to stay. When I tell him three months, he comments,

'They may like to stay longer.' And he awards them a six-month visitor's permit. He also adds, 'I wish I had met someone like you when I was a young lad.'

He asks if I will make a point of seeing him when we return to the airport so that the girls can tell him of the good time that they are obviously going to have.

Two minutes after he leaves my side the girls run into the arrivals lounge and the smile on their faces is worth any money I have spent on their expenses. I'll remember the hugs they give me as long as I live.

Several days later I receive an e-mail from Trev bluntly telling me not to return to *Antinea* but without any explanation as to his decision. So I begin a new phase of life that is to change me forever.

Ofa, Eseta and I have a wonderful holiday exploring the British Isles and visiting my sons and most things come up to my expectations though one of my sons still has reservations, maybe because he thinks that I am trying to replace his mother. I could never do that, it would be impossible.

The three months is up; despite the generosity of the immigration officer allowing them a six-month visa I have decided enough is enough and we once more return to Manchester airport. I have booked three flights to New Zealand where I have also arranged for us to have another month's vacation before returning them safely to their mother in Tonga as I had promised.

The relationship with Eseta and Ofa has, I know by my gut feelings, gone as far as it can, so even though I am staying with their family in Tonga I am, in reality, alone again.

Chapter 23

Manu and Arthur 'It's a Match'

It is while staying with Ofa and Eseta's family that I meet Manu. She lives in the next house and we meet virtually over the garden fence, where we sometimes exchange pleasantries about the weather or make small talk about England or Tonga and our differing cultures.

Our acquaintance progresses to firm friendship and soon develops into love. In her I find the soul mate I've been looking for and Manu agrees that she feels the same way. A few weeks later we fly to England together where we bond into a very happy and fulfilling relationship. Manu settles well into the way of life and the very different culture in England but under the rules of her visa has to leave England to return to Tonga after six months.

The time passes all too quickly in a rapid haze of joy and I ask her to marry me; a proposal she delightedly answers yes to. Manu is to be my wife and I couldn't be happier.

The plan is to return together to Tonga for six months where her two small sons still live and then apply for another visa for Manu to re-visit England. On her return here we intend to marry. But the best laid plans…

Ultimately we decide it is better to marry in Tonga so that her two boys, Vave, aged ten, and Nau, aged five, can be present along with her immediate family. Our traditional Tongan wedding takes place on the twenty-ninth of January 2004 after we have been together for a year.

Both Manu and I wear tavalas, which are hand-decorated rush skirts. The boys do too and the ceremony takes place in Nuka Alofa church after which we return to Manu's home for a family wedding feast of roast pig, root vegetables and tropical fruit.

During our long honeymoon my new sons, Vave and Nau, and I get to know each other well. Together we have been on fishing trips and camping excursions to neighbouring islands, enjoying quality time together as a family.

It is now April and this is to be our final camping trip on the Isle of Atata before Manu and I return to England to prepare for Vave and Nau joining us. I take a long last look at my beautiful surroundings, breathe deeply to taste the pure air and inhale the sweet scent of the wild flowers in the background of tropical forests. I listen intently to the music of the sea lapping on the reef and to the voices of Manu, Vave and Nau as they make the most of our last few minutes by playing together on the beach. Bending I pick up a handful of the finely sifted, white coral sand and let it dribble slowly through my fingers; watching it fall I reflect on the sands of time.

Taking the opportunity to embark on the adventure of sailing the Pacific was the second wise and big decision I made in my life. The first was asking Iris to be my wife; asking Manu to marry me was the third. How many men are blessed enough to be able to marry a second wonderful wife after having forty years of wedded bliss with their first sweetheart?

As I have said before, I was born lucky.

* * *